1999 Update

to accompany

The Law of
Public
Communication

Fourth Edition

Kent R. Middleton
University of Georgia

Robert Trager
University of Colorado

 LONGMAN

An Imprint of Addison Wesley Longman, Inc.

New York • Reading, Massachusetts • Menlo Park, California • Harlow, England
Don Mills, Ontario • Sydney • Mexico City • Madrid • Amsterdam

1999 Update to accompany *The Law of Public Communication, Fourth Edition.*

Copyright © 1999 by Addison Wesley Longman, Inc.

Please visit our website at http://longman.awl.com

ISBN: 0-8013-3278-8

2345678910 - VG - 01009998

PREFACE

The *1999 Update* to *The Law of Public Communication* discusses several significant developments in media law since the fourth edition was published. In 1997, the Supreme Court delivered an important ruling that the Internet should be regulated rather loosely, like newspapers, not under the tighter regulatory scheme imposed on broadcasting. The Court's Internet decision, discussed in chapter 13 of the *1999 Update,* struck down the Communications Decency Act, a federal statute barring indecency on the word-wide computer network. In another important telecommunication decision, the Supreme Court ruled Congress may require cable operators to carry the signals of local broadcast stations. In 1998, the Supreme Court said public television stations may exclude less newsworthy political candidates from debates if the candidates are not excluded because of their views.

In the two years since *The Law of Public Communication* was published Congress passed the *Electronic Freedom of Information Act*, expanding public access to digital government information. EFOIA is discussed in chapter 11. In the privacy chapter, we discuss a number of cases in which the media's newsgathering techniques are leading to rulings that reporters intrude and trespass. Intellectual property cases recounted in chapter 5 help define lawful use of advertising and trademarks on the Internet and the rights of publishers to place freelancers' works in digital databases. Chapter 3 reports the lucrative libel settlements with two media outlets by former Olympic bombing suspect Richard Jewell. The libel chapter also discusses law defining liability for defamation on the Internet, and the case in which Oprah Winfrey evaded liability for disparaging Texas cattle.

In 1998, the Supreme Court said Congress could require the National Endowment for the Arts to consider whether artistic projects are decent, show respect for diverse beliefs, and comply with general standards of decency before funding the projects. In the area of corporate speech, the Supreme Court issued rulings on insider trading and campaign spending by political parties. Several other developments affect the advertising of tobacco and casinos.

Like earlier editions of the *Update*, the 1999 edition parallels the textbook, *The Law of Public Communication*. The subject headings in the *Update* are the same as the headings in the textbook. The table of contents and text of the *Update* indicate precisely where new legal developments should be inserted in the textbook.

Longman issues an *Update* each year between new editions of the text. Professors who adopt the fourth edition of *The Law of Public Communication* receive a copy of the *1999 Update* directly from the publisher. Students buying a new copy of the text will receive the *1999 Update* with the text at no additional charge. Professors may also order copies of the *1999 Update* for sale in campus bookstores. A test bank for use with the text is available to instructors from Longman at no cost. Also available to instructors and students is *Key Cases in the Law of Public Communication*, a supplementary reader containing significant cases discussed in the text.

With the *1998 Update*, Professor Robert Trager, associate dean for graduate studies in the School of Journalism and Mass Communication, University of Colorado, joins Professor Kent Middleton of the University of Georgia. Professor Bill Chamberlin, who founded *The Law of Public Communication* with Middleton more than a decade ago, leaves the enterprise to devote more time to research and administration as eminent scholar of journalism and director of the Brechner Center for Freedom of Information at the University of Flordia. His vision, dedication, and skill will be sorely missed. Also departing with our regret after the fourth edition is Matthew Bunker, professor of journalism at the University of Alabama, who wrote the fourth edition with Middleton and Chamberlin. We pledge to try to maintain the high standards of Chamberlin and Bunker for accuracy, completeness, and readability.

We would like to thank Jeanne Chamberlin for exacting editing and proof reading over many editions of *The Law of Public Communication* and its updates. For the *1999 Update* we would also like to thank Jennifer Wilson, a Master's candidate at the University of Georgia, and the staff of the law library at the University of Colorado. Finally, we thank the numerous professors and students who have used and commented on the four editions of *The Law of Public Communication*. We welcome comments that enable us to meet the needs of students and faculty studying the rapidly changing field of communication law.

Kent R. Middleton
Robert Trager

CONTENTS

1

PUBLIC COMMUNICATION
AND THE LAW

William J. Brennan, who wrote many influential opinions during a long tenure on the Supreme Court, died in 1997.

THE COURTS

The Federal System

The U.S. Supreme Court

(*Insert before "The State Systems," p. 14*) On July 24, 1997, William J. Brennan Jr., one of the most influential justices of the Supreme Court, died at age 91. A liberal force on the Court for 34 years, Brennan had retired in 1990 after writing some 1,350 opinions. During his long career, he wrote majority opinions furthering voting rights, desegregation, freedom of expression, freedom of religion, and criminal due process. In 1964 he wrote the Court's opinion in the landmark libel case of New York Times v. Sullivan, ruling that the media are not liable for publishing false statements about public officials unless the statements are published with actual malice. In 1989 he wrote the Court's opinion in a case upholding the First Amendment right of a citizen to burn the American flag as a form of political protest.

In a speech in 1987, Justice Brennan said he believed the Constitution exists to guarantee "the essential dignity and worth of each individual." Judges, he said, must be proficient at more than "logical analysis." Judges interpreting the constitution, he said, must "be sensitive to the balance of reason and passion that mark a given age, and the ways in which that balance leaves its mark on the everyday exchanges between government and citizen."

2

THE FIRST AMENDMENT

The Supreme Court delivered several important First Amendment decisions since the fourth edition of *The Law of Public Communication* was published. Among them are cases involving the Internet and advertising, cases that will be discussed in other sections of the Update. In a picketing case summarized here, the Court upheld a 15-foot buffer between abortion protesters and entrances to abortion clinics. In an important college press case, a federal court upheld the power of a state university to seize class yearbooks. In the meantime, high schools are cracking down on off campus publications.

WHO IS PROTECTED

Student Expression

(*Insert after first complete paragraph, p. 55*) Several high schools are cracking down on off campus student publications, some of which are not disruptive. The school district in McKinney, Texas, suspended Aaron Smith for a day and told him to take down the web site he created at home for "Chihuahua Haters." Earlier, the school district in Bellevue, Washington, withdrew backing for a National Merit Scholar because the district disliked the parody of the high school newspaper that the student created on a home web page.[1] In Georgia, Statesboro High School

---

[1]Tamar Lewin, "A New Free Speech Battle for Students," *New York Times*, Mar. 8, 1998, at 13.

suspended the creator and contributors of a crude web site critical of the principal and the school.[2] In Miami, nine high school students were arrested on charges of hate crimes for publishing racist language and suggesting violence in an underground booklet.[3] The school board argued the district would be harmed by having to endure a "demonstrably disruptive student" if the system could not expel Boucher.

The U.S. Court of Appeals for the Seventh Circuit upheld a Wisconsin school district that wanted to expel a student for publishing an underground newspaper that the court said was disruptive. An article by Justin Boucher in *The Last*, a paper distributed at Greenfield High School near Milwaukee, told students how to hack the school's "gay ass computers."[4] The article also described how to enter the high school computer setup utility, figure out passwords and see lists of student and faculty users.

Overturning a lower court, the court of appeals allowed the school district to proceed to expel Boucher. Enjoining the expulsion, as a lower court had, would undermine the authority of the school board "to take disciplinary action for what it believed to be a serious threat to school property," the appeals court said. School officials had reason to believe that Boucher's newspaper would be disruptive, the court said, because the school found evidence of tampering with computers and because the newspaper encouraged students to follow a blueprint for invading Greenfield's computer system. Even though the paper was produced off campus, the court said it was "student" expression because the article was distributed on campus and advocated on-campus activity.

(*Insert at bottom of p. 55*) In Kentucky, a federal court for the first time used the Supreme Court's *Hazelwood* decision, permitting restrictions on the high school

---

[2]*Id.*

[3]"Students Are Arrested Over A Racist Book," *New York Times*, Feb. 27, 1998, at A17.

[4]Boucher v. School Bd., 134 F.3d 821, 26 Media L. Rep. 1394 (7th Cir. 1998).

press, as precedent for censoring a college student publication.[5] The federal district court for the Eastern District of Kentucky upheld officials' confiscation of student yearbooks at Kentucky State University. The court said the administration acted reasonably when it withheld distribution of the yearbook because the publication did not include school colors, did not appropriately identify Kentucky State students and contained much information unrelated to the university. It was reasonable, the court said, for the university administration to require the yearbook to focus on Kentucky State and to explain who appeared in yearbook pictures. The court ruled that the administration needed only to justify its regulations as reasonable because the yearbook was not a public forum. Because the yearbook was not a public forum, the university was not required to show that disruption would ensue if the university failed to censor.

No court had previously upheld the constitutionality of a state university censoring student publications on the easily met standard of "reasonableness." Quoting *Hazelwood*, the Supreme Court case allowing reasonable regulations only on the high school press, the Kentucky court said a university, like a high school, may refuse to disseminate student speech that does not meet high standards of quality set by the school. Four months later, the court refused to alter or vacate its decision.[6]

The court did not say whether the university administration might similarly censor the campus newspaper. Students at the campus paper complained because the administration removed an adviser at the paper. But the court ruled Kentucky students had no First Amendment claim against the university for censoring the campus newspaper because the administration cut no stories, halted distribution of no editions and reinstated the advisor who had been temporarily removed.

---

[5]Kincaid v. Gibson, Civ. No. 95-98 (E.D. Ky., Nov. 14, 1997).

[6]Kincaid v. Gibson, Civ. 95-98 (E.D. Ky., Mar. 5, 1998).

CONTENT-NEUTRAL REGULATIONS

Narrow Tailoring

(Insert after second full paragraph, p. 70) Similarly, the Supreme Court in 1997 upheld an injunction prohibiting abortion protesters from demonstrating within 15 feet of the entrances to abortion clinics and their parking lots. In Schenck v. Pro-Choice Network of Western New York,[7] the Court ruled that the government's interests justified an appropriately tailored injunction allowing women unimpeded access to abortion clinics in Rochester and Buffalo, New York. The government's interests were ensuring public safety and order, promoting the free flow of traffic on streets and sidewalks, protecting property rights, and protecting a woman's freedom to seek services related to their pregnancies. Protesters had been marching, kneeling, sitting, and laying in clinic doorways and driveways to block access by patients and clinic employees.

The Court, split 6-3, upheld the 15-foot "fixed buffer zones," including a provision that allowed two pro-life "counselors" within the zones providing they ceased counseling if requested to by persons entering the clinics. The Court also voted 8-1 to strike down a portion of the injunction establishing "floating buffer zones." Abortion protesters in these zones were allowed to talk to patients and employees approaching the clinics, providing the protesters remained at least 15 feet from persons as they walked or drove to the abortion facilities. The Court said the floating buffers restricted too much speech because they prohibited protesters from communicating messages from a normal conversational distance and from handing out leaflets on the public sidewalks.

---

[7]519 U.S. 357 (1997).

3

LIBEL

Television celebrity Oprah Winfrey escaped liability for disparaging Texas cattle, but statutes punishing false statements about perishable foods remain in many states. The media again are enduring large awards, particularly for punitive damages, in libel and privacy suits. But appellate courts often reverse or reduce large awards against the media. Two media settled libel suits from Richard Jewell, once a suspect in the bombing during the Olympic games, but Jewell pursues a libel suit in Atlanta. A federal court ruled that Internet providers are not responsible for defamation posted on electronic bulletin boards by third parties.

Large damage awards remain a problem for media, according to a study of libel and privacy cases. The Libel Defense Resource Center (LDRC) reported in 1997 that damages awarded against media defendants in 1996 in libel and privacy cases averaged almost $3 million, with awards in more than half of the cases exceeding $1 million.[1] The percentage of awards exceeding $1 million was the highest since the LDRC began monitoring awards in 1980. Punitive damages were up sharply, the LDRC said, rising to an average award of $2.8 million in 1996, more than double the average punitive award of $1.2 million in 1994 and 1995.

---

[1]"News Notes: Average Libel, Privacy Award Is $3 Million, Survey Notes," 25 Media L. Rep. (BNA), Mar. 11, 1997.

In December 1996, a federal jury in Florida awarded Bank Atlantic and its chief executive officer $10 million for an ABC broadcast saying the bank misled investors in securities transactions, an award that a federal judge refused to throw out.[2] In 1997, the U.S. Supreme Court refused to review a $1 million award against ABC over a 1992 story on "World News Tonight with Peter Jennings" in which the network reported that a machine designed to recycle garbage "does not work."[3] The lower courts treated the manufacturer of the recycling machine as a private figure because the company did not inject itself into the recycling controversy. ABC argued the manufacturer should be considered a public figure because it promoted its product to local government as a solution to a preexisting controversy.[4]

In Houston, a federal judge threw out a $200 million libel award for punitive damages against Dow Jones & Company, publisher of the *Wall Street Journal*, but let stand a $22.7 million award for actual damages.[5] The judge reversed the $200 million award, the largest punitive damage award to date, for lack of actual malice. A Houston jury in March 1997 found that the *Journal* published five false, defamatory statements about a brokerage firm that went out of business a month after the article was published. Dow Jones said the article "chronicled, but did not cause" the collapse of the brokerage firm.

In December 1996, NBC reached a settlement, reportedly for more than $500,000, with Richard Jewell, the suspect exonerated in the bombing of Olympic Centennial

---

[2]"The Big Numbers of 1996," *Nat'l Law J.*, Feb. 10, 1997, at C6; Mary Hladky, "Libel Verdict Against ABC Should Stand, Judge Rules," *Broward Daily Business Rev.*, July 18, 1997, at B1.

[3]Lundell Mnfg. Co. v. American Broadcasting Co., 98 F.3d 351, 25 Media L. Rep.(BNA) 1001 (8th Cir. 1996), *cert. denied* 117 S. Ct. 1470 (1997).

[4]"News Notes: ABC Requests Review of Defamation Verdict," 25 Media L. Rep. (BNA), Ap. 22, 1997.

[5]Edwin McDowell, "Award Is Cut in Dow Jones Libel Case," *New York Times*, May 24, 1997, at 21.

Park in Atlanta.[6] The settlement included no apology or retraction by NBC. Jewell claimed on-air statements by anchor Tom Brokaw concluded that Jewell set off the bomb in Olympic Centennial Park that killed one. Jewell also settled with CNN for an undisclosed amount of money.

However, Jewell filed a libel suit against the *Atlanta Journal-Constitution,* which broke the story – based on unidentified sources – that Jewell was a suspect in the bombing. Jewell said the *Journal-Constitution* libeled him when it reported that he fit the profile of a "lone bomber" and compared him to Wayne Williams, who was convicted of killing children in Atlanta in the 1970s.[7] In 1998, the *Journal-Constitution* was contesting a judge's order to reveal its sources for the Jewell story. (*See Update, chapter 10*)

PLAINTIFF'S BURDEN OF PROOF

Defamation

Product Disparagement or Trade Libel

(Insert before "Character, Habits, and Obligations," p. 85) In a highly publicized case, a federal district judge in Texas ruled that Texas cattlemen could not sue television talk-show celebrity Oprah Winfrey under a Texas food disparagement statute. The Texas statute, like statutes in more than a dozen other states, make the media liable if they knowingly disseminate false information about a perishable food product being unsafe. Winfrey was sued over an April 1996 broadcast in which she vowed never to eat another hamburger. Winfrey's proclamation followed warnings by experts on her television show that the deadly Mad Cow Disease could migrate from Britain to the United States. Sales of beef dropped after Winfrey's show, causing Texas cattlemen to sue.

---

[6]Kevin Sack, "Atlanta Papers Are Sued in Olympic Bombing Case," *New York Times,* Jan. 29, 1997, at 12.

[7]"News Notes: Former Bombing Suspect Sues Atlanta Newspaper for Libel," 25 Media L. Rep. (BNA), Feb. 11, 1997.

The federal judge in Texas ruled that Texas cattlemen could not sue Winfrey under the Texas statute because cattle are not "perishable." Unlike peaches and other perishable fruits and vegetables, cattle do not spoil if false statements about their safety cause sales to diminish. Following a trial determining common law disparagement, a jury ruled that Winfrey had not published false statements about Texas cattle.[8]

While the media won the Texas case, the media were not able to challenge the constitutionality of the Texas statute. The Texas law, and so-called "veggie libel statutes" in other states, are vulnerable to constitutional attack because they inhibit food critics, environmental writers and agricultural experts who criticize how American foods are grown and processed. While the First Amendment protects wide-open debates on public issues--debates in which experts often disagree--the veggie libel statutes make critics liable for large payments unless their statements are based on scientific fact. However, environmentalists, biologists, agronomists, geneticists and other scientists often disagree over the safest methods for producing and processing food. The media are likely to challenge laws requiring that statements in public debates be based on "facts" which are themselves disputed.

Publication

(Insert before "Summary," p. 99) Even if an Internet provider does not try to control the content of electronic bulletin boards, Section 230 of the Telecommunications Act of 1996 prohibits suits against Internet providers for libel placed on their systems by third parties. A federal appeals panel upheld a ruling in 1997 that Section 230 bars a libel suit against an Internet service provider over third-party postings, even if the service provider is notified that libelous material has been posted.

---

[8]See, "Agricultural Disparagement Laws: The Trend to Impose Statutory Liability on Speech," *Libel Defense Resource Center Bulletin*, April 30, 1998.

In the case, America Online was sued by Kenneth Zeran over anonymous Internet advertisements for tee shirts, advertisements linking Zeran to offensive messages about the bombing of the Alfred P. Murrah Federal Building in Oklahoma City.[9] One advertisement said, "Visit Oklahoma. . . It's a BLAST!!!" Another proclaimed, "McVeigh for President 1996." Readers were invited to call "Ken" at Kenneth Zeran's phone number in Seattle. Zeran, a commercial publisher with no connection to the Oklahoma City bombings, tried to sue America Online for negligently allowing libelous material to appear on its bulletin board, even after Zeran asked that it be removed. Zeran received many abusive phone calls after AOL disseminated the bogus advertisements.

Ruling for America Online, the federal court said the Telecommunications Act of 1996, which prohibits treating Internet providers as "publishers" when third parties post electronic messages, preempts state law, thus barring a libel suit against AOL. Freedom of expression would be chilled, the court said, if online service providers were saddled with the "staggering" task of reviewing the millions of interactive messages disseminated daily on their electronic networks. An equally impossible burden would be placed on electronic service providers if they were held responsible for removing libelous messages after being "notified" of their presence, the court concluded. "In light of the vast amount of speech communicated through interactive computer services," the court said, "these notices could produce an impossible burden for service providers, who would be faced with ceaseless choices of suppressing controversial speech or sustaining prohibitive liability."

---

[9]Zeran v. America Online, Inc., 129 F.3d 327, 25 Media L. Rep. (BNA) 2526 (4th Cir. 1997), *cert. denied*, 1998 U.S. LEXIS 4047 (1998).

4

PRIVACY AND PERSONAL SECURITY

Newsgathering techniques continue to present challenging trespass and privacy suits against the media. A federal appeals court ruled the media act as law enforcement officials exceeding the terms of a search warrant when they coordinate searches with officials. A North Carolina jury awarded the Food Lion supermarket chain $5.5 million from ABC for fraud and trespass the network employed to produce an inside story about unsanitary meat, but a judge greatly reduced the award. The California Supreme Court allowed an accident victim to sue a television crew that videotaped her treatment in an emergency medical helicopter. In Arizona, a federal court ruled a trial should be held to determine whether secret recording in a workplace was for "criminal or tortious" purposes. A federal appeals court has allowed parents to sue ABC, claiming an "outrageous" secret taping of their son caused his death by returning him to alcohol. A federal court in Ohio ruled that a purveyor of commercial e-mail trespassed on the property of an Internet provider. Congress was considering legislation to curb "paparazzi."

But a California appeals court threw out a $1.2 million judgment awarded employees who were secretly videotaped at work, and two federal courts have ruled that officials do not invade citizens' privacy when they invite journalists to accompany them when they serve a warrant in a private place. ABC did not invade the privacy of a flight attendant when the network interviewed her in the doorway of her home. A federal appellate court ruled that a trial should be held to see if publishers of a guide book for "hit men" should be liable for murders. The Clinton administration continues to seek controls on exports of encryption technology and promotes software allowing access to encrypted transmissions by law enforcement officials.

Privacy continues to be an important issue of federal policy. In May, 1998, President Bill Clinton called for stronger privacy policies in government agencies. The next day, Vice President Al Gore called for greater protection of consumer and medical privacy. Some 40 privacy bills were pending in Congress as public opinion polls revealed that Americans are concerned about retaining control about personal information.[1] Of particular concern is protection of electronic information that can be assembled easily and disseminated rapidly and broadly.

Earlier the president issued an executive order on cryptography, forbidding the export of encryption technology that could harm national security or foreign policy, even if foreign competitors already sell comparable products. People who make encryption software available electronically are given the difficult task of preventing "the unauthorized transfer" outside the United States.[2] However, in December 1996, a federal judge in California declared unconstitutional a Cold War law that prohibited the export of encryption technology. The decision allows Daniel J. Bernstein, Research Assistant Professor at the University of Illinois at Chicago, to disseminate encryption instructions without registering with the government as an arms dealer as required by the Arms Export Control Act.[3]

Judge Marilyn Hall Patel said the registration requirements of the Arms Export Control Act constituted an unconstitutional prior restraint on protected speech. Citing the Pentagon Papers case (see text, pp. 60-61), Judge Patel said that Bernstein's computer source code is constitutionally protected expression for

---

[1]Nina Bernstein, "Proposals to Protect Privacy Seem to Face Stalemate in Contradictory Goals," New York Times, Oct. 20, 1997, at A12.

[2]A detailed analysis of the Clinton policy and more information on the Executive Order is available at: http://www.epic.org/crypto/export_controls.

[3]Bernstein v. United States, 945 F. Supp. 1279 (N.D. Calif. 1996); see also, Karn v. Dept. of State, 107 F.3d 923 (D.C. Cir. 1997).

which the government cannot require a license simply by invoking the need to protect national security. The judge said the law was unconstitutionally vague because it did not adequately define the information banned from export. Judge Patel also ruled the law lacked due process because it failed to provide for a time limit on the licensing decision, required no prompt judicial review and required too little of the government to defend the denial of a license.

Producers of encryption software, the media, and some members of Congress continue to argue that American software companies should be able to compete with foreign producers of encryption software. The administration continues to argue for encryption legislation requiring that electronic transmissions be accessible to law enforcement officers possessing a software "key" that can be matched, when authorized, to keys held by other parties. The administration argues the encryption technology with keyed access will allow the government to monitor the electronic transmissions of terrorists and commercial lawbreakers. But civil libertarians counter that people and businesses using the Internet should be able to choose from powerful, commercial encryption software allowing them to protect privacy, prove the authenticity of transactions, and improve computer security.

In March 1998, the FBI told phone companies to prepare the ability to conduct thousands of wiretaps at once. The increased wiretapping capabilities would allow the FBI to implement the Communications Assistance to Law Enforcement Act of 1994.[4]

INTRUSION, TRESPASS, AND CIVIL RIGHTS VIOLATIONS

Intrusion into Public and Quasi-Public Places

(*Insert before "Summary," p. 177*) A committee of the House of Representatives held hearings in late May, 1998, on two bills to curb paparazzi, whose aggressive newsgathering techniques have been vehemently condemned since Diana, Princess of Wales, died in a car crash as she was chased by photographers in Paris. One bill

---

[4] "FBI and Telephone Industry Working Toward Wiretap Agreement," Electronic Privacy Information Center, March 9, 1998 .

would make it a federal crime to "harass" people or trespass for the purpose of photographing or recording them for commercial gain. The bill would also prohibit the use of "a visual or auditory enhancement device" to capture images and sounds that otherwise could not be recorded without trespassing.

Intrusion into Private Places

(*Insert before "Third Party Monitoring," p. 177*) The California Supreme Court ruled in June 1998 that an accident victim could bring an intrusion suit against a broadcast production company that filmed the victim in a medical helicopter and recorded her conversations with a nurse.[5] Affirming a lower court, the California high court ruled that Group W Productions may have intruded into the privacy of the accident victim, Ruth Shulman, by recording her conversations with a nurse at the accident scene and videotaping and recording her in the rescue helicopter. A journalist was invited into the helicopter by Mercy Air, operator of the rescue service. The nurse attending to Shulman transmitted the conversations from a wireless microphone.

The court agreed with Group W that Shulman had no claim for the disclosure of embarrassing private facts. The court concluded that broadcast of Shulman's identity, injuries and conversations were not embarrassing invasions of privacy, but were truthful, relevant additions to a newsworthy video documentary about medical evacuations from accident scenes.

While the broadcast did not reveal embarrassing facts, the court said a jury should decide whether Group W intruded on a zone of privacy that Shulman might reasonably expect in the medical helicopter, much as patients in a hospital room or ambulance have an expectation that they will not be photographed or their conversations with doctors and nurses recorded. "It is neither the custom nor the habit of our society that any member of the public at large or its media representatives may hitch a ride in an ambulance and ogle as paramedics care for an injured stranger," the court said.

---

[5]Shulman v. Group W Productions, Inc., 1998 Cal. LEXIS 3190, June 1, 1998.

A jury might even conclude that Group W intruded at the accident scene by recording conversations between Shulman and the nurse, the court said. While it would not be intrusive for any bystander to videotape the accident in plain view near a highway, the court noted, Group W was able to record conversations between Shulman and the nurse only because the nurse wore a transmitter allowing Group W access to intimate medical conversations. "A patient's conversation with a provider of medical care in the course of treatment, including emergency treatment, carries a traditional and legally well-established expectation of privacy," the court said.

Participant Monitoring

Federal Law

(*Insert after second full paragraph, p. 179*) A federal court in Arizona refused to dismiss a case against ABC in which a medical testing laboratory charged PrimeTime Live with secretly recording "for the purpose of committing any criminal or tortious act." The court said a jury should decide whether ABC secretly recorded conversations about how lab technicians conducted tests for pap smears for illegal as well as legal purposes. The lab claimed ABC recorded the conversations not only for lawful newsgathering but also for unlawful defamation, intrusion, and theft of trade secrets.[6]

State Prohibitions

(*Substitute for two paragraphs before "Secret Recording as a Tort, p. 181*) In February 1997, a California appeals court threw out the $1.2 million judgment won by employees of a psychic marketer for secretly videotaping their workplace conversations. The appellate court ruled that the employees lacked a reasonable expectation of privacy in a workplace conversation.[7] However, the U.S. Court of

---

[6]Medical Laboratory Management Consultants v. ABC, Inc., 25 Media L. Rep. 1724 (D. Ariz. 1997).

[7]Sanders v. American Broadcasting Co., 52 Cal. App. 4th 543, 60 Cal. Rptr. 2d 595 (1997), *rev. granted*, 1997 Cal. LEXIS 2812, May 20, 1997.

Appeals for the Ninth Circuit ruled that the parents of one of the psychic marketing employees could sue ABC under California law for outrageous conduct causing the death of their son. The parents, Frank and Stefa Kersis, charge that the broadcast of the secret taping of their son, Highland, so distressed him that he returned to alcohol which eventually killed him.[8] In another case, the Ninth Circuit affirmed summary judgment for ABC, which was sued for secretly taping a conversation with a flight attendant who served O.J. Simpson as he flew from Los Angeles to Chicago the night Simpson's former wife was murdered.[9] The Ninth Circuit ruled that the attendant, Beverly Deteresa, had no legitimate expectation of privacy when she voluntarily talked to an ABC producer at the door of her California condominium while the broadcaster secretly taped the conversation.

Trespass

(Insert before "Accompanying Officials," p. 184) After evidence was presented at trial, a jury in Greensboro, N.C., awarded Food Lion $5.5 million for trespass and fraud by ABC, sending the media a sharp warning about undercover newsgathering. The jury awarded Food Lion the extensive punitive damages for the ABC employees' trespassing into nonpublic areas under false pretenses and fraudulently concealing their identities on their job applications. The two ABC producers also violated a legal duty of loyalty to their supermarket employer. Shortly after the jury award, a federal district court reduced the punitive damage award to $315,000.[10] The court said the ratio of punitive damages to actual damages ($1,400) was so high that it violated due process.

---

[8]Kersis v. American Broadcasting Companies, 103 F.3d 139 (9th Cir. 1996), full text at 1996 U.S. App. LEXIS 30329.

[9] Deteresa v. American Broadcasting Co, 121 F.3d 460, 25 Media L. Rep.(BNA) 2038 (9th Cir. 1997), cert. denied, 1998 U.S. LEXIS 3448, May 26, 1998.

[10] Food Lion , Inc. v. Capital Cities/ABC, Inc., 984 F. Supp. 923, 25 Media L. Rep. (BNA) 2185 (M.D.N.C., 1997).

The jury awarded Food Lion only $1,400 actual damages to reimburse the supermarket chain for the costs of training and paying two ABC producers who were briefly employed by the company.[11] By limiting actual damages to $1,400, the court refused to allow Food Lion to collect for lost sales, lost profits and a diminished stock price following the broadcast.[12] The court said Food Lion's losses were not the result of ABC's trespass, fraud and breech of duty. The broadcast itself was not on trial in the suit over newsgathering practices.

A federal court in the Midwest has extended trespass law to the Internet. The Federal District Court for the Southern District of Ohio enjoined an advertiser from trespassing on Compuserve's proprietary computers by sending unsolicited "junk mail" to Compuserve customers. The federal court said mass electronic mailings by Cyber Promotions, Inc., hurt Compuserve by burdening its computers and causing irritated subscribers to abandon the Internet provider. When Compuserve consented to transmit e-mail messages, it retained authority to deny access to unauthorized parties, the court said.[13] In other filings, America Online has asserted that unauthorized companies transmitting unsolicited e-mail with false header information trespass and violate the federal Computer Fraud and Abuse Act.[14]

Accompanying Officials

(Insert before "Receiving Stolen Information," p. 185) After *Ayeni*, a least two federal courts ruled that officials do not violate the Fourth Amendment if they

---

[11]Barry Meier, "Jury Says ABC Owes Damages of $5.5 Million," *New York Times*, Jan. 23, 1997, at 1; Scott Andron, "Food Lion versus ABC," *Quill*, Mar. 1997, at 15.

[12]Food Lion, Inc. v. Capital Cities/ABC Inc., 964 F. Supp. 956, 25 Media Law Rep. 1856 (M.D.N.C. 1997).

[13] CompuServe, Inc. v. Cyber Promotions, Inc., 962 F. Supp. 1015, 25 Media L. Rep.(BNA) 1545 (1997).

[14] "News Notes: AOL Asserts 'Spammers' Violate Computer Fraud Act," 25 Media Law Rep. (BNA) Nov. 11, 1997.

invite journalists to observe and report on lawful searches. The U.S. Court of Appeals for the Fourth Circuit ruled that federal and state officers did not violate the privacy of Charles and Geraldine Wilson when the officers allowed two *Washington Post* reporters to observe and photograph an early-morning confrontation in 1992 as officers attempted to execute a warrant for the arrest of the Wilsons' son. The *Post* photographer took pictures of Charles Wilson, dressed only in undershorts, held face down on the floor of his home, and of his wife in a sheer nightgown.[15]

Reversing the district court, the full Fourth Circuit Court of Appeals ruled the officers were entitled to qualified immunity because the law in 1992 did not clearly establish that officers would violate citizens' constitutional rights by allowing media to accompany them into a private residence. Officials are immune from privacy suits unless they are plainly incompetent or knowingly violate the law, the court said. Immunity protects officers from "bad guesses in gray areas." The Fourth Circuit disagreed with the Second Circuit's statement in *Ayeni* that officers "obviously" violate the Fourth Amendment when they allow journalists to accompany them into the home.

Also distancing itself from the *Ayeni* ruling, the Eighth Circuit ruled that neither St. Louis police nor KSDK television violated the Fourth Amendment when police allowed a television crew to film the search for weapons in a home. The police did not violate clearly established constitutional principles of which they should have been aware, the court said.[16] The court noted that *Ayeni* was decided after the St. Louis search. But, even so, the court said it is not "self-evident that the police offend general fourth-amendment principles when they allow members of the news media to enter someone's house during the execution of a search warrant." Furthermore, the court said the journalists were not acting under color of law when they accompanied police. "KSDK acted independently of the police in deciding to enter the house and videotape the events," the court said. "Neither KSDK nor the police assisted the other."

---

[15]Wilson v. Layne, 114 F.3d 111 (4th Cir. 1997).

[16]Parker v. Boyer, 93 F.3d 445, 24 Media L. Rep. 2307 (8th Cir. 1996), *cert. denied*, 117 S. Ct. 1081 (1997).

However, the Ninth Circuit has ruled that officials violate the Fourth Amendment and journalists act under color of law when a search is coordinated with the media and the news media's taping and recording do not contribute to the search. The Ninth Circuit ruled that federal officials and CNN violated the Fourth Amendment rights of a Montana couple when CNN cameras and a microphone accompanied officials on a search of the couple's ranch. The court ruled United States Fish and Wildlife agents and CNN violated the privacy of 71-year old Paul Berger and his wife, Erma, 81, when agents with a warrant searched the couple's ranch near Jordan, Montana, for evidence that Berger was illegally poisoning eagles. CNN cameras mounted in federal vehicles taped agents as they searched the Bergers' property outside their home. Conversations inside the home were transmitted to CNN recorders from a microphone worn by agent Joel Scrafford.

Earlier, CNN signed an agreement in which the U.S. District Attorney's office agreed to CNN's participation if the cable operator refrained from telecasting any videotape until a defendant's rights to a fair trial had been secured.[17] The media wanted footage for their environmental programs and the government wanted to publicize its efforts to combat environmental crime. Paul Berger was acquitted of all charges except for failing to follow the label when using a toxic chemical.

As in *Ayeni*, the Ninth Circuit ruled that authorities exceed the scope of their search warrants when officials authorize the presence of media cameras and microphones. The cameras mounted in federal vehicles violated the Bergers' privacy in their land and farm buildings, the court said. The hidden microphone violated the privacy of the Bergers' home during agent Scrafford's interview there. The search warrant did not provide for a search of the Bergers' house.

The court viewed CNN as a commercial entertainment medium whose presence at the Bergers' property was unrelated to law enforcement. Media representatives themselves were liable as government actors, the court said, because they closely planned the search with authorities—including a written contract—and conducted the search "to enhance its entertainment, rather than its law enforcement value." In

---

[17]Berger v. Hanlon, 129 F.3d 505, 25 Media L. Rep.(BNA) 2505 (9th Cir. 1997).

no other cases, the court said, "did law enforcement officials engage in conduct approaching the planning, cooperation and assistance to the media that occurred in this case." The court remanded the case to see if CNN could also be liable for trespass and infliction of emotional distress.

EMOTIONAL DISTRESS AND PERSONAL INJURY

Physical Harm

Incitement

(Insert before "Negligence," p. 213) A federal appeals court has ruled that a publisher might be liable for disseminating a book that teaches how to be a successful murderer. The U.S. Court of Appeals for the Fourth Circuit reversed summary judgment for Paladin Enterprises, ruling that the First Amendment does not protect expression that intentionally aids and abets a criminal act. Paladin is the publisher of *Hit Man: A Technical Manual for Independent Contractors*, a book relied upon by a James Perry as a guide when he murdered three members of a family.[18] Relatives of the family sued Paladin for aiding and abetting murders by contract. *Hit Man* openly taught would-be killers how a professional "gets assignments, creates a false identity, makes a disposable silencer, leaves the scene without a trace, watches his mark unobserved and more." Perry followed *Hit Man* closely, even shooting his victims through the eyes, as the book advised.

The court rejected Paladin's claim that *Hit Man* was constitutionally protected speech because it did not incite anyone to murder. The Fourth Circuit overturned a district court decision that was supported by numerous mainstream publishers and broadcasters. The district court ruled that that the Supreme Court's decision in *Brandenburg v. Ohio* (*see text, p. 41*) barred liability for Paladin because the book only "advocated" or "taught" lawlessness, but was not "directed to inciting or producing imminent lawless action."

---

[18] Rice v. Paladin Enters, Inc., 128 F.3d 233, 25 Media L. Rep.(BNA) 2441 (4th Cir. 1997), *cert. denied,* 118 S. Ct. 1515 (1998)..

However, the Fourth Circuit determined that while *Brandenburg* protects "abstract" teaching, it does not protect the intentional, detailed direction of murderers the court found in *Hit Man*. Paladin's book was not constitutionally protected, the Fourth Circuit said, because the publisher "intended that *Hit Man* would immediately be used by criminals and would-be criminals in the solicitation, planning, and commission of murder and murder for hire."

To the Fourth Circuit, *Hit Man* constitutes the "archetypal example" of speech which deserve no First Amendment protection because it "methodically and comprehensively prepares and steels its audience to specific criminal conduct through exhaustively detailed instructions on the planning, commission, and concealment of criminal conducts." The court said that few other publications describing potentially illegal activities would be unprotected by the First Amendment because few other publishers would demonstrate the specific intent to aid criminality that Paladin demonstrated.

5

INTELLECTUAL PROPERTY

President Clinton signed a statute in 1997 allowing criminal prosecutions for willful copying when the copier has no profit motive. A federal district court ruled that newspaper and magazine publishers may reproduce works on CD-ROM and in databases without paying freelance writers extra compensation. A federal appeals court ruled that a company electronically reporting sports scores gleaned from broadcasts does not misappropriate facts belonging to sponsors of broadcast sporting events. The Sixth Circuit Court of Appeals ruled that professors' course packs infringe the copyright of journal and book publishers. Another federal appeals court ruled that a book attempting to parody Dr. Seuss' *The Cat in the Hat* was a copyright infringement. An Internet company has agreed to cease "framing" web pages of news companies in the Internet company's own images and advertisements. Trademark owners are stopping Internet providers from using their trademarks as Internet domain names. Two international treaties were signed in late 1996 to increase the minimum level of protection for copyrighted works around the world and to adapt international copyright law to global digital network environments like the Internet.

COPYRIGHT

Rights

Distribution

(Insert before "Performance and Display," p. 230) In August 1997, freelancers lost their attempt to control publishers' use of their work on CD-ROMs and databases. A federal district court in New York ruled that the *New York Times* and other publishers could market the printed work of their freelancers on CD-ROM or commercial databases without permission of the freelancers and without paying them extra.[1]

The court ruled that publishers are not creating a new work for which they should pay royalties when they reproduce a printed work on CD-ROM or add it to a commercial database. The CD-ROM and database versions are essentially the same work, the court said. "Those technologies preserve that element within electronic systems which permit users to consult defendants' periodicals in new ways and with new efficiency, but for the same purposes that they might otherwise review the hard copy versions of those periodicals," the court said.

The court said the CD-ROM and database versions of published articles are analogous to microfiche copies of newspapers and magazines. Courts have ruled that publications do not create new works requiring new royalty payments when they archive newspapers and magazines on microfiche or microfilm. The *Tasini* case supported publishers' common demand that freelance writers and photographers sign contracts assigning all rights to publishers.

---

[1]Tasini v. New York Times Co., 972 F. Supp. 804, 25 Media L. Rep. (BNA) 2057 (S.D.N.Y. 1997), *reconsideration denied*, 981 F. Supp. 841 (S.D.N.Y. 1998).

Denying Tasini's motion to reconsider, the district court said that placing the articles in a database preserved the same originality and editorial discretion in digital format that publishers demonstrated when they published the original newspapers and magazines. Although articles may not be housed sequentially and contiguously in a database, a database still constitutes a version of the original, the court said, because the electronic system carries the publisher's complete selection of articles identified by the periodicals in which they appeared. Not only are all the articles of the collection in the database, but when displayed electronically, they are displayed with headers identifying the hard copy periodicals in which they originally appeared. They appear with text, title, author, publication and date.

The court did not say whether freelancers should be compensated when their work is distributed on the Internet. But, presumably, publishers that can disseminate published works through CD-ROMs and commercial databases may also disseminate them from a database serving the Internet.[2]

Infringement

(*Insert before "Access," p. 235*) In late 1996, the United States and more than 120 other countries negotiated two new international treaties to increase protection for copyrighted works in the traditional physical world as well as in cyberspace.[3] Under the auspices of the World Intellectual Property Organization (WIPO), a special United Nations agency, the countries adopted the treaties to build upon the protection guaranteed under the Berne Convention[4] and the World Trade Organization TRIPs Agreement.[5]

---

[2] Briefs were filed on appeal in February, 1998. "News Notes: Writers Ask CA2 to Protect On-Line Publication of Works,", 26 Media L. Rep.(BNA), Mar. 10, 1998.

[3] *See* WIPO Copyright Treaty and WIPO Performances and Phonograms Treaty (available at .

[4] The Berne Convention for the Protection of Literary and Artistic Works (Paris Text) was last updated in 1971.

[5] The Agreement on Trade-Related Aspects of Intellectual Property Rights came into effect on January 1, 1995.

The WIPO treaties reiterate and reinforce rights of copyright owners under the Berne Convention and the TRIPs Agreement by requiring countries that join the treaties to grant authors the basic rights of reproduction, communication to the public and adaptation, as well as the right to prevent the commercial rental of computer programs and musical recordings. In addition, the treaties require member countries to grant a distribution right, the copyright owner's exclusive right to sell or otherwise disseminate copies of a work to the public. To bring international copyright law into the digital era, the treaties also guarantee that copyright owners will have the exclusive right to make their works available online. This "making available" right will ensure that copyright owners will be able to prevent the unauthorized posting or transmission of their musical recordings, motion pictures, computer programs and other copyrighted works on or through computer networks, such as the Internet.

In addition, both treaties require member countries to prohibit circumvention of technological measures, such as encryption, used to protect copyrighted works against unauthorized access or use. The treaties also allow countries to adopt certain exceptions to the rights required under the treaties, such as fair use. A third treaty, which would have required countries to grant separate protection for the effort expended to create databases, was never discussed. WIPO is expected to begin informal discussions of a database treaty in November 1998.

It is hoped the two WIPO treaties adopted in 1996 will stem foreign copyright piracy, which is estimated to cost American computer software, motion picture, music and other copyright industries nearly $15 billion each year.[6] As of July 1998, the U.S. Senate had passed the implementing legislation required for the United States to join the treaties, and similar legislation was under consideration in the House of Representatives.[7] The treaties will come into force when 30 countries ratify them.

---

[6]The International Intellectual Property Alliance piracy report is available at http://www.iipa.com.

[7]See S. 2037, 105th Cong., 2d Sess. (passed May 14, 1998); H.R. 2281, 105th Cong., 2d Sess. (1998).

(*Insert at bottom of p. 336*) President Clinton signed a law in 1997 making it a criminal offense to willfully infringe a copyright causing at last $10,000 harm, even if no one intends to profit financially. The law, the "No Electronic Theft Act," closed a loophole in the copyright statute that barred criminal prosecutions if unauthorized copying was not motivated by profit.[8] In 1994, a federal court ruled the federal government could not prosecute a college student who gained nothing when he allowed subscribers to his electronic bulletin board to copy more than $1 million of software free.[9] The new law would allow prosecution of the student even though he had no profit motive when he allowed others to copy.

Fair Use

Purpose and Character of the Use

Parody

(*Insert before "Teaching and Noncommercial Research, p. 240*") A federal appeals court in 1997 upheld an injunction barring distribution of *The Cat NOT in the Hat!*, rejecting the publisher's claim that the book was a constitutionally protected parody of the famous book, *The Cat in the Hat* by Dr. Seuss.[10] *The Cat NOT in the Hat!* was about the murder of OJ Simpson's former wife, Nicole, and her friend, Ron Goldman. The court ruled *The Cat NOT in the Hat* appropriated Dr. Seuss' cat in a stove-pipe hat, a narrator named "Dr. Juice," and the rhyming style of Dr. Seuss:

---

[8]Pub. L. No. 105-147; 111 Stat. 2678 (1997).

[9]United States v. LaMacchia, 871 F. Supp. 535 (D. Mass. 1994).

[10]Dr. Seuss Enterprises v. Penguin Books USA, Inc., 109 F.3d 1394, 25 Media Law Rep. 1641 (9th Cir. 1997).

JUSTICE
Hmm . . . take the word JUICE.
Then add ST.
Between the U and I, you see.
And then you have JUSTICE.
Or maybe you don't.
Maybe we will.
And maybe we won't.

The court said *The Cat NOT in the Hat!* failed to transform the Dr. Seuss book into new expression; it failed to conjure up the original, but rather imitated it. The court said *The Cat NOT in the Hat!* did not ridicule or criticize Dr. Seuss' book, but merely retold the tale of the Simpson murder in a manner mimicking Dr. Seuss. The court disagreed that the so-called parody evoked the mixture of frivolousness and moral gravity of *The Cat in the Hat*, thereby commenting on society's reaction to the Brown-Goldman murders. "Pure shtick," said the court of the fair use argument presented by the publishers of *The Cat NOT in the Hat*.

Effect upon the Plaintiff's Potential Market

(*Substitute paragraph beginning at the bottom of page 244*) On rehearing, a federal appellate court reversed itself, ruling that photocopying of professors' course packs is a copyright infringement. The U.S. Court of Appeals for the Sixth Circuit ruled, as the Second Circuit had in the Kinkos case, that unauthorized production of professors' course packs damages the market or potential market of the publishers who own the copyrights.[11]

---

[11] Princeton University Press v. Michigan Document Services, Inc., 99 F.3d 1381 (6th Cir. 1996), *cert. denied,* 117 S. Ct. 1336 (1997).

UNFAIR COMPETITION

Misappropriation

(*Insert at bottom of p. 248*) A federal appeals court in New York ruled in 1997 that electronics companies do not misappropriate property of the National Basketball Association when they provide "real time" scores and statistics of professional sporting events. The U.S. Court of Appeals for the Second Circuit removed an injunction against Motorola, manufacturer of a hand-held pager that displays sports scores, and Sports Team Analysis and Tracking Systems (STATS), which transmits sports scores gathered by STATS employees from television and radio broadcasts. The court rejected the NBA's claim that the SportsTrax paging service should be enjoined from gathering and transmitting free information from NBA games and broadcasts and from competing with a similar electronic sports service that the NBA plans to offer.[12]

The court said STATS would misappropriate information if it stole time-sensitive factual information, thus threatening the existence of a competitor. But the court said STATS employees did not steal information from a competitor, but rather collected the statistical facts through their own efforts and expense from television and radio broadcasts.

In its misappropriation decision, the Second Circuit agreed with a lower court ruling that the NBA had no copyright in facts about games in progress, because sporting events are not "authored." Unlike a play or opera, the court said, competitive athletic events have no underlying expression or script. Even planned aspects of sport, such as the T formation in football and a spin in ice skating, are not copyrightable works of authorship, the court noted, but are techniques available for other competitors to attempt. While videotapes of sporting events are copyrightable, the games themselves-- including scores and statistics generated during the games--are not. "Motorola and STATS did not infringe NBA's

---

[12]National Basketball Ass'n v. Motorola, Inc., 105 F.3d 814, 25 Media L. Rep. 1385 (2d Cir. 1997).

copyright because they reproduced only facts from the broadcasts, not the expression or description of the game that constitutes the broadcast."

Trademarks

Infringement

(*Insert before "First Amendment," p. 252*) In June 1997, Total News, Inc., which operates an Internet news site, agreed to discontinue making it appear that *The Washington Post* and other prominent news sources were associated with *Total News* on the *World Wide Web*.[13] *Total News* agreed to stop "framing" web pages belonging to the *Post, CNN* and other news sources with the *Total News* name and advertising. In a trademark and copyright infringement suit,[14] The *Post, Cable News Network,* the *Wall Street Journal* and other news organizations claimed that *Total News* pirated their products and reduced the value of their business by presenting their web pages diminished and partially obscured by the *Total News* frame. The news organizations argued the public would be confused when they saw the companies' news and advertising under the *Total News* name next to *Total News* advertising.

In the settlement, *Total News* agreed to avoid any practices that are "likely to imply" *Total News* is affiliated with the *Post, CNN* or the other news organizations. Visitors to the *Total News* site will still be able to jump to the web pages of the news organizations by clicking on plain text hyperlinks. But the news organizations' pages will appear with no names or advertising associated with *Total News.*

---

[13]"Settlement Halts Internet Framing and Permits Text-Only Hyperlinking," 54 *Pat., Trademark & Copright J.* (BNA) 165 (June 19, 1997).

[14]Washington Post Co. v. Total News, Inc., 97 Civ. 1190 (S.D.N.Y., filed Feb. 20, 1997).

Dilution

(Insert before "Abandonment," p. 255) A growing number of dilution and infringement claims are resulting from the unauthorized use of trademarks as Internet domain names. Domain names tell Internet users where an individual or company is located in cyberspace. Sometimes the names are used in an unsavory context. A federal judge in Washington enjoined a company from using the domain name, "candyland.com," to identify a sexually explicit web site. The Hasbro company, manufacturer of children's toys and games and owner of the "Candy Land" trademark, argued successfully that the value of its mark was being diminished.[15] Similarly, Toys R Us, the well-known toy store chain, convinced a federal judge to enjoin use of the name, "Adults R Us," to identify a web site for adult entertainment.[16] Domain names are issued by Network Solutions, Inc., under contract with the National Science Foundation. Network Solutions used to award domain names on a first-come first-served bases, but is now allowing trademark owners to contest the assignments. In May 1997, more than 50 Internet providers and telecommunications companies signed a memorandum in Switzerland calling for the United Nations to oversee registration of Internet domain names.[17]

---

[15]Hasbro, Inc. v. Internet Entertainment Group, Ltd., 40 U.S.P.Q.2d (BNA) 1479 (W.D. Wash. 1996).

[16]Toys "R" Us, Inc. v. Akkaoui, 40 U.S.P.Q.2d (BNA) 1836 (N.D. Calif. 1996).

[17]"Internet Registration; Agreement Will Allow More Groups to Issue Addresses," *Chicago Tribune*, May 2, 1997, at Business 2. Settlement Halts Internet Framing and Permits Text-Only Hyperlinking," 54 *Pat., Trademark & Copyright J.* (BNA) 165 (June 19, 1997).

6

CORPORATE SPEECH

The Supreme Court ruled that traders violate the securities laws by buying or selling a company's stock based on confidential information, even if traders have no direct connection with the company. The Court decided that the federal election law does not limit the amount of money a political party may spend on advertising in a campaign, if the party has not yet selected its candidate to run in the general election. In 1998, Congress again failed to adopt campaign reform legislation. Also, the Supreme Court found that a law requiring California fruit growers to contribute to a fund used for generic advertising does not constitute unconstitutional compelled speech. A federal district court held that advertisers and advertising agencies have no right to use an Internet service provider's system without permission. A federal appellate court said preventing dentists from advertising prices and quality illegally inhibited competition.

REFERENDA AND OTHER PUBLIC ISSUES

Freedom from Compelled Speech

(Insert before "Summary," p. 262) Just as corporations need not disseminate messages they oppose, a federal district court held that on-line service providers need not carry commercial material on the Internet for advertising agencies. A

federal court in Pennsylvania held that America Online (AOL) had the right to prevent Cyber Promotions, an Internet advertising agency, from sending 1.9 million of its clients' ads per day to AOL subscribers without paying AOL or obtaining AOL's permission.[1]

The court held that because AOL is a private company, not a government agency, the First Amendment does not require AOL to open its system to all comers. Merely because the Internet is widely used does not mean an on-line service provider is a "public system" that must provide access to everyone, according to the court. The court said that by refusing to allow Cyber Promotions to send its advertisements, AOL was protecting its computers, which are AOL's own property. But, the court said, AOL's refusal did not limit Cyber Promotions' access to the Internet. For example, it could reach AOL subscribers through mail, television, and newspapers, the court said. Also, the court said, AOL has a system allowing AOL's subscribers to receive only the advertisements they want. Cyber Promotions could send its messages by that method under a contract with AOL.

In another case involving Cyber Promotions, a federal court in Ohio ruled that the on-line advertising agency trespassed when it used CompuServe's on-line system without permission.

The Supreme Court ruled that a federal law requiring fruit growers to pay for advertising did not unconstitutionally compel speech. Nothing in the law, the Court said in 1997, requires fruit growers and marketers to speak when they would rather not, or respond to messages with which they disagree. The Court therefore refused to strike down a 1937 law requiring fruit growers to contribute to a fund to urge consumers to buy fruit.

The Court rejected claims from California peach, plum, and nectarine growers that the law unconstitutionally forced them to pay for advertising, even though they

---

[1] Cyber Promotions Inc. v. America Online Inc., 948 F. Supp. 436, 24 Media L. Rep. (BNA) 2505 (E.D. Pa. 1996).

preferred to advertise on their own. The farmers also argued that they could not change the ads, even when they disagreed with them.

The Supreme Court ruled that the law raises no First Amendment questions, even though it requires advertising that growers cannot control. The Court said fruit growers are not required "to communicate any message to any audience," or support "any political or ideological views."

Further, the Court said the ads create no "crisis of conscience" because the growers presumably agree with the advertising, which urges people to purchase peaches, plums and nectarines. The Court said its earlier decisions allowed groups to require collective funding of messages even when some members of the group objected, as long as the messages were pertinent to the group's general purpose. Here, the statute organized a fruit growers' collective to urge people to purchase their produce. None of the ads promoted name brands.

The Court found it unnecessary to test the constitutionality of the advertising regulation because the Court ruled it to be an economic regulation — not a speech regulation — within Congress' power.

A federal appellate court would not allow the California Dental Association to require dentists advertising their prices as "low" or "reasonable" to include substantiating information in their advertisements.[2] The U.S. Court of Appeals for the Ninth Circuit said compelling dentists to prove lower prices in their advertisements would make price-based advertising impossible.

The association also said its member dentists could not advertise their quality, safety, and comfort because these claims cannot be verified and therefore may be misleading. The court said this restriction prevented dentists from competing on the basis of service rather than price. The court said the association's rules artificially limited competition among dentists in violation of federal antitrust laws.

---

[2] California Dental Association v. Federal Trade Commission, 128 F.3d 720 (9th Cir. 1997), *petition for cert. filed* (April 3, 1998).

The court said the association's goal of prohibiting misleading advertising did not justify banning all price and quality claims.

ELECTIONS

Permitted Election Communications

(Insert before "Issues, Organizations, and Voter Registration," p. 266) In 1998, Congress once again rejected campaign reform. The Senate failed to end a Republican filibuster against Sen. John McCain's (R-Ariz.) and Sen. Russell D. Feingold's (D-Wis.) reform bill. In late summer of 1998, the House of representatives continued debates over amendments to Rep. Christopher Shays' (R-Conn.) and Rep. Martin T. Meehan's (D-Mass) bill, similar to the McCain-Feingold legislation.[3] Observers gave the House bill little chance of passage.

Both bills proposed banning "soft money," currently unregulated contributions to political parties that are spent for get-out-the-vote campaigns and other purposes not directly related to electing candidates. The bills also would restrict interest group advertising within two months before elections.

(Insert before "Political Action Committees," p. 267) The Supreme Court ruled political parties may purchase unlimited advertising to support candidates if the parties do not coordinate that spending with the candidates. The Colorado Republican Party did not violate the Federal Election Campaign Act's spending limits by purchasing radio ads attacking a Democrat running for the U.S. Senate, the Court said.[4] If the party had coordinated spending with a candidate, that would constitute a "contribution" which the Supreme Court earlier ruled may be limited.

---

[3] Alison Mitchell, "G.O.P. Leadership in House Rebuffed on Election Funds," *New York Times,* June 20, 1998, at 1.

[4] Colorado Republican Fed. Campaign Comm. v. Federal Election Comm'n, 518 U.S. 604 (1996).

The Colorado Republican Party bought radio advertising time before it chose a candidate to run in the general election for the United States Senate. Because no Republican senatorial candidate had been selected, the Court said there was no one with whom the party could "coordinate" its ad campaign. Therefore, the party's expenditures were "independent," and did not violate the law by exceeding limits on contributions to candidates.

Because the expenditures were independent, the Court majority said it did not need to consider the constitutionality of the federal election law's limitation on a political party's spending that is coordinated with candidates. Three justices — Chief Justice Rehnquist and Justices Kennedy and Scalia — wanted the Court to face that question, arguing Congress could limit such campaign spending.

As in *Buckley v. Valeo* (discussed on pages 269, 270 and 272), the Court was faced with balancing the government's goal of preventing real or perceived election corruption — allowing someone to "buy" an election — against candidates' and political parties' First Amendment rights to express themselves. It decided a political party's independent expenditures — not coordinated with a candidate's campaign — could not be limited.

SECURITIES TRANSACTIONS

Fraud

Duty to Disclose Insider Trading

(Insert before "Investment Advisers," p. 292) Others Possessing Nonpublic Information People using confidential information to buy or sell securities violate the insider trading laws, even if the traders have no direct association with the company whose shares they trade, the U.S. Supreme Court ruled. The Court said a company owns its nonpublic information just as it does the rest of its property, and the information is for the company's exclusive use. A person violates the securities laws by misappropriating insider information, such as the unpublished fact that a company is targeted for a takeover.

In *United States v. O'Hagan*,[5] the Court ruled James O'Hagan misappropriated information belonging to his Minneapolis law firm when he bought shares of the Pillsbury Company before the flour miller was purchased by a British company. O'Hagan's firm represented Grand Metropolitan PLC (Grand Met), a British company, which hired a Minneapolis law firm to represent it while considering its takeover bid for the Pillsbury. Pillsbury's share value increased dramatically when Grand Met announced it would bid for the company. O'Hagan sold his shares for a profit of more than $4.3 million.

Although O'Hagan was not involved directed in representing Grand Met, he was convicted of violating securities, federal mail fraud, and money laundering laws. The United States Court of Appeals for the Eighth Circuit reversed the convictions, but the Supreme Court disagreed.

The Court said in addition to the "traditional" theory of insider trading, applicable when, for example, a company director or officer uses nonpublic information to trade in the company's stock, there is a second approach — the "misappropriation" theory. As in the Winans case (see text, p. 293), a person violates securities laws when she or he "misappropriates confidential information for securities trading purposes in breach of a duty owed to the source of the information."

In the *Grand Met* case, O'Hagan did not represent Grand Met, but his law firm did. The firm's connection allowed O'Hagan to learn nonpublic information — that Grand Met intended to make a bid for Pillsbury. It also created a fiduciary responsibility for him to let Grand Met know he would use that information to purchase Pillsbury stock, or to refrain from buying the stock. Since he did neither, he misappropriated Grand Met's information to trade in Pillsbury's stock, and in doing so, violated insider trading laws. The Court noted, however, if O'Hagan had found in a park trash can information about Grand Met's takeover plans, he would have no fiduciary duty. He could trade freely in Pillsbury stock.

---

[5] 117 S. Ct. 2199 (1997).

The duty not to misappropriate information the Court found in the *Grand Met* decision is the same as found in the *Carpenter v. United States* case (see text, p. 293) in which a *Wall Street Journal* reporter misappropriated information belonging to the newspaper. He gave that information to another person who used it to trade securities. Neither the reporter nor the trader had a connection with the company whose securities were traded. The reporter and others involved were convicted of mail and wire fraud.

7

ADVERTISING

Congress refused to approve an agreement between the tobacco industry and forty state attorneys general which would have limited tobacco advertising and required the industry to fund anti-smoking campaigns. Four states have reached agreements with the tobacco industry which include marketing and advertising limitations. A federal appellate court upheld laws banning billboards advertising alcohol and tobacco products in areas where children likely would see them. Two federal appellate courts disagreed about whether a federal law forbidding the mailing or broadcasting of advertisements for casino gambling directly advances the government's interest in reducing social problems caused by gambling, and a federal district court allowed broadcasters to carry casino advertising.

If commercial advertisements on city busses appropriate a mayor's identity, the mayor may sue but the city may not halt the ads, a federal appellate court ruled. A federal appellate court said satisfying the public's interest in whether dairy cows ingested a growth hormone was not a sufficient government interest to justify requiring milk producers to label their products. A federal appellate court held attorneys may use direct mail to solicit clients among criminal and traffic defendants.

The Federal Trade Commission said parents must be notified before a company collects personal information from children over the Internet, and parents must consent to a company giving Internet-collected information about children to others. The FTC affirmed goods carrying a "Made in the U.S.A." label must be "all or virtually all" made in this country. An FTC judge refused to order corrective advertising for an eight-year, $55 million deceptive advertising campaign.

FIRST AMENDMENT AND ADVERTISING

Four-Part Test

Legitimate Government Regulatory Interest

(Insert before "Direct Advancement of the Government's Regulatory Interest," p. 310) Although the government once easily could show a substantial interest in regulating advertising, courts often now demand a strong showing that the government's interest is a substantial one. The U.S. Court of Appeals for the Second Circuit said the government lacked sufficient grounds to require milk labels to reveal whether cows were given a growth hormone.[1] The court overturned a Vermont law requiring labels on dairy products to inform customers if the products were made with milk from cows using the genetically engineered bovine growth hormone rBST. The court ruled the statute violated milk producers' First Amendment rights by requiring them to include information on dairy product cartons against their will. It might have found the law constitutional, the court said, if the government's interest had been the public's health or safety. However, the federal Food and Drug Administration has determined rBST does not pose a health danger, although some consumer groups disagree.

Another federal appellate court ruled a state had no legitimate interest in barring attorneys from sending direct mail solicitations to criminal and traffic defendants within 30 days of their arrest.[2] The U.S. Court of Appeals for the Fourth Circuit said such mailings do not influence recipients to hire lawyers who sent the letters any more than a newspaper advertisement would. Also, the court said a lawyer's letter directed to an individual who has been charged with a crime or traffic

---

[1]International Dairy Foods Assoc'n v.. Amestoy, 92 F.3d 67, 24 Media L. Rep. (BNA) 2089 (2d Cir. 1996).

[2] Ficker v. Curran, 119 F.3d 1150, 25 Media L. Rep. (BNA) 2049 (4th Cir. 1997).

letter directed to an individual who has been charged with a crime or traffic violation will invade someone's privacy as little as a letter addressed to "occupant." The court said there is no reason to delay letters to criminal suspects, unlike the delay of lawyer letters to accident victims, upholding the U.S. Supreme Court (see *Florida Bar,* text p. 309). Someone arrested for a crime or charged with a traffic violation may need a lawyer quickly, the Fourth Circuit said.

Direct Advancement of the Government's Regulatory Interest

(Insert after second complete paragraph, p. 311) Following the U.S. Supreme Court's lead in *Rubin* and *44 Liquormart* (see text, p. 311), lower courts have demanded more evidence than was shown in *Posadas* that a government regulation will directly advance a government interest. In 1997, the U.S. Court of Appeals for the Ninth Circuit said a federal law banning casino advertising was unconstitutional because there was insufficient evidence the ban would advance government interests in reducing gambling.[3] The court said a ban on casino ads would not reduce gambling because some casino advertising still would be permitted. An exception in the law allows advertising of casino gambling run by Native American tribes under federal law permitting casinos on tribal reservations. The court said it would be difficult to reduce gambling's social problems by banning advertising of other casino gaming if tribal casinos can advertise. Since the government argued its interest was to lessen social problems gambling causes, yet the law permits the advertising of certain forms of casino gambling, the statute does not pass the *Central Hudson* test, said the court.

The Ninth Circuit disagreed with an earlier decision in which the U.S. Court of Appeals for the Fifth Circuit, relying on *Posadas,* found the government's goal of reducing the social ills connected with casino gambling was substantial.[4] The court held the law directly furthered the government's interest. Since advertising is intended to "increase consumer demand," reducing advertising for casinos will

---

[3] Valley Broadcasting Co. v. United States, 107 F.3d 1328, 25 Media L. Rep. (BNA) 1363 (9th Cir. 1997), *cert. denied,* 118 S. Ct. 1050 (1998).

[4] Greater New Orleans Broadcasting Assoc. v. United States, 69 F.3d 1296, 24 Media L. Rep. (BNA) 1146 (5th Cir. 1995), *vacated and remanded,* 117 S. Ct. 39 (1996).

diminish the number of people gambling at them, said the court. It also said there was a reasonable fit between the statute and the government's interests because there were no less restrictive ways to achieve the government's goal. However, the Supreme Court directed the Fifth Circuit to reconsider its decision based on *44 Liquormart.*

The Fifth Circuit recognized the advertising exception for tribal casinos. However, the court said Congress properly could decide the social benefits of permitting tribal casinos to advertise were greater than the social costs of that particular form of casino advertising.

Before the U.S. Supreme Court refused to review the Ninth Circuit's ruling finding unconstitutional the federal ban on most casino advertising,[5] a federal district court permitted broadcast stations to begin carrying casino ads by for-profit companies. [6] The federal law overturned by the Ninth Circuit ,but upheld by the Fifth Circuit, prohibits casino or lottery advertising on broadcast stations except advertising for casinos operated by Native American tribes and lotteries run by a state, a non-profit organization, the government, or a company which does not have gambling as its primary business.

Narrowly Drawn Ban

(Insert after second complete paragraph, p. 313) The U.S. Court of Appeals for the Fourth Circuit upheld Baltimore ordinances restricting outdoor advertising of alcoholic products and cigarettes. The city banned such billboards in areas where children might be exposed to the messages, such as close to school grounds and neighborhood play areas. The Fourth Circuit had upheld these laws a year before the Supreme Court handed down *44 Liquormart,* in which the Court struck down

---

[5] Valley Broadcasting Co. v. United States, 107 F.3d 1328, 25 Media L. Rep. (BNA) 1363 (9th Cir. 1997), *cert. denied,* 118 S. Ct. 1050 (1998).

[6] Players International, Inc. v. United States, 988 F. Supp. 497, 26 Media L. Rep. (BNA) 1266 (D.N.J. 1997).

a law prohibiting price advertising where liquor is sold[7] (discussed on pages 311, 312-313). However, the Supreme Court told the Fourth Circuit to reconsider its decisions in light of *44 Liquormart*. The lower court did so, but came to the same conclusion — the laws are constitutional.[8]

The Fourth Circuit accepted Baltimore's reasons why the ban on billboards in areas frequented by children was a "reasonable fit" with the city's goal of reducing underage drinking and smoking. First, the regulation was aimed at protecting children, who cannot use the products legally. The Supreme Court often has agreed the government has a legitimate interest in protecting children in ways not applicable to adults, such as limiting children's access to indecent cable, radio, and over-the-air television programming (see Chapters 12 and 13), and to non-obscene print media (see Chapter 8). Second, the city left many alternative forms of communication for alcohol and cigarette companies to advertise their products, including magazines, newspapers, direct mail, and billboards where children would be less likely to see them. Third, the city was not attempting to make the products illegal or unavailable for those permitted to use them. For these reasons, the court found the ordinances did not infringe First Amendment rights more than necessary, and were sufficiently narrowly drawn to meet the fourth prong of the commercial speech test.

(Insert before "Summary," p. 313) Congress seemingly has rejected broad bans on tobacco companies' advertising and marketing, constitutionally suspect because they are not narrowly drawn restrictions. However, the advertising and marketing limitations are incorporated into four states' agreements with the tobacco industry.

---

[7] Anheuser-Busch, Inc. v. Schmoke, 63 F.3d 1305, 23 Media L. Rep. (BNA) 2357 (4th Cir. 1995), *vacated and remanded,* 116 S. Ct. 1821 (1996); Penn Advertising of Baltimore v. Mayor and City Council of Baltimore, 63 F.3d 1318, 23 Media L. Rep. (BNA) 2367 (4th Cir. 1995), *vacated and remanded,* 116 S. Ct. 2575 (1996).

[8] Anheuser-Busch, Inc. v. Schmoke, 101 F.3d 325 (4th Cir. 1996), *cert. denied,* 117 S. Ct. 1569 (1997)); Penn Advertising of Baltimore v. Mayor and City Council of Baltimore, 101 F.3d 332 (4th Cir. 1996), *cert. denied,* 117 S. Ct. 1569 (1997).

In June 1998, the U.S. Senate rejected a bill introduced by Sen. John McCain (R-Ariz.) that included sweeping tobacco advertising restrictions: (1) no outdoor advertising, (2) no humans or cartoon characters in advertisements, (3) no Internet advertising, (4) limits on using tobacco brands in television shows and motion pictures, (5) no advertising where tobacco products are sold, (6) only black and white text ads in newspapers and magazines having more than 25 percent youth readership, and (7) specified formats and contents in health warnings on packages and in advertisements.

McCain's bill was based on a June 1997 agreement between the tobacco industry, forty state attorneys general, and a group of attorneys. That deal, which would have limited damages awarded against tobacco companies, required congressional approval. The McCain bill's defeat likely means Congress will not approve the 1997 agreement.

Forty states have sued the tobacco industry claiming, among other things, the states paid out millions of dollars in health care for smokers. Four states — Florida, Minnesota, Mississippi, and Texas — have settled their suits, with tobacco companies agreeing to pay the states approximately $35 billion. These settlements contain advertising and marketing restrictions, including forbidding tobacco ads on billboards near schools, tobacco companies financing anti-smoking campaigns, prohibiting tobacco product advertising at sports events and on public transportation, and banning cartoon characters in tobacco advertisements.

Anti-tobacco advocates have expressed particular concern about underage smoking. Some argued R. J. Reynolds' cartoon character Joe Camel caught young people's attention and persuaded them to smoke. The FTC voted 3-2 in 1997 that Joe Camel enticed youth to begin smoking. In July 1997 Reynolds announced it no longer would use Joe Camel in the company's advertising and marketing.

The McCain bill included annual surveys of underage smokers to ascertain what cigarette brands they smoke. Companies manufacturing those products would have been penalized financially if there was no decrease in the number of young people smoking their brands. After the bill was defeated, President Clinton announced in June 1998 he would issue an executive order requiring the government to conduct annual surveys of young smokers.

Earlier, the United States Food and Drug Administration (FDA) claimed jurisdiction over tobacco advertising and marketing, arguing tobacco was a drug. A federal district court ruled Congress did not give the FDA power to control tobacco company advertising.[9] That decision is on appeal to the United States Court of Appeals for the Fourth Circuit.

Forbidding advertisements is not a narrowly drawn way to achieve government goals, the U.S. Court of Appeals for the Second Circuit said in 1998. The court said banning an advertisement is an unconstitutionally broad method of preventing appropriation.[10] The court said if New York City Mayor Rudolph Giuliani believed his name was being used without permission in an advertisement on the city's busses, he could sue the advertiser for appropriation (see text, pp. 196-200). But the city may not refuse to carry the advertisements on their busses, the court said.

New York Magazine and New York's Metropolitan Transit Authority (MTA) contracted to place the magazine's ads on the side of city buses. The ads included the magazine's logo and read, "Possibly the only good thing in New York Rudy hasn't taken credit for." "Rudy" is Giuliani's nickname. Giuliani complained to the MTA he had not given New York Magazine permission to use his name for commercial purposes. The MTA then refused to carry the ads.

The appellate court said the advertisement was both a commercial attempt to sell magazines and a constitutionally-protected political commentary. In either case, the court said, the city had no grounds for the prior restraint. If a political statement, the ad posed no imminent danger justifying prior restraint (see text, pp. 58-59). If commercial speech, the ad could be regulated only if the MTA's action was narrowly tailored to achieve the government's goal. A prior restraint is more

---

[9] Coyne Beahm Inc. v. United States Food and Drug Administration, 966 F. Supp. 1374 (M.D.N.C. 1997).

[10] New York Magazine v. Metropolitan Transportation Authority, 136 F.3d 123, 26 Media L. Rep. (BNA) 1301 (2d Cir. 1998), *petition for cert. filed* (June 15, 1998).

extensive than necessary to achieve the government's purpose of barring unauthorized commercial appropriation, the court said.

UNFAIR AND DECEPTIVE ADVERTISING

Deception

Reasonable Consumer

(Insert after second complete paragraph, p. 317) Companies using the Internet to collect information from children must tell parents how the information will be used and obtain parental consent before releasing the data to anyone else, according to the Federal Trade Commission (FTC).[11] In 1997 the FTC said businesses must direct a clear notice to parents before collecting personally identifiable information — such as name, address, telephone number, and e-mail address — from children.

Also, parents must be notified if children are told the information is collected online for one reason but the information also is used for a different purpose. For example, a web site might tell children completing a questionnaire they can earn points toward obtaining a premium. The web operator must tell parents if the information the children supply is used for marketing purposes. Failure to notify parents is deceptive under the Federal Trade Commission Act, [12] according to the FTC.

The FTC said it is not sufficient for a web operator to tell children to ask their parents if information may be used for commercial purposes. Notice must be directed to the parent. The notice should state who is collecting the information, what information is being collected, to whom and in what form the data will be revealed, and how parents may prevent the information being disclosed.

---

[11] Letter from Jodie Bernstein, Director, Bureau of Consumer Protection, Federal Trade Commission, to Kathryn C. Montgomery, President, Center for Media Education, July 15, 1997, available at <http://www.ftc.gov/os/9707/cenmed.htm>.

[12] 15 U.S.C. § 45.

The FTC also said a business may not misrepresent a product being advertised on its web site. For example, the web site may not say the business independently evaluated a product and chose to put product information on the site if the product mention in fact is a paid advertisement. The FTC said this would be a deceptive practice under the Federal Trade Commission Act.

Express Falsehoods

(Insert before "Implied Falsehoods," p. 319) A "Made in the U.S.A." product label will continue to mean what it has for more than 50 years. In December 1997 the FTC ruled only a product "all or virtually all" made in the United States could carry the label.[13] Putting a "Made in the U.S.A." label on a product not meeting the "all or virtually all" definition would be a false statement under FTC rules. The FTC had considered allowing products 75 percent made in this country to carry the "Made in the U.S.A." label.

FEDERAL REMEDIES

Required Statements

Corrective Advertising

(Insert before "Competitor Remedies," p. 335) A Federal Trade Commission administrative law judge refused to order corrective advertising as a remedy for false commercials running for eight years and costing $55 million.[14] The judge said the advertising campaign for Doan's Pills was not effective enough to warrant corrective advertising.

---

[13] Robert D. Hershey, Jr., "F.T.C. Drops Plan to Ease Standard of 'Made in U.S.A.,'" *New York Times,* Dec. 2, 1997, at 1.

[14] Noartis Corp., 1998 FTC LEXIS 24 (March 9, 1998) (administrative law judge).

The manufacturer of Doan's Pills claimed in broadcast ads its product provided better relief for back pain than did other analgesics. One television commercial showed a Doan's package in front of Advil, Extra Strength Tylenol, and Bayer packages. A voice-over said, "New Extra Strength Doan's is made for back pain relief," and said Doan's contained an ingredient the other products lacked.

FTC rules require claims of health product superiority to be substantiated by two clinical studies. Doan's manufacturer had no clinical studies proving the drug's superiority. The FTC staff asked the judge to order the company not to run the ads and also to air corrective ads.

The judge issued a cease and desist order forbidding claims of Doan's superiority. However, the FTC judge said Doan's false ads did not justify requiring corrective advertising, which is an extraordinary remedy, because the campaign was comparatively short and ineffective. The judge said the only litigated case in which the FTC had required corrective advertising involved Listerine's false claims in ads running more than four decades (see text, pp. 334-335), much longer than the eight years Doan's commercials ran. Also, the judge said, the Doan's campaign was not very effective. Evidence showed consumers did not remember Doan's superiority claim two or three days after seeing a Doan's commercial. Also, the judge said, the advertising campaign did not significantly increase Doan's sales.

8

OBSCENITY

The Supreme Court ruled Congress could require the National Endowment for the Arts to consider standards of decency and respect for diverse beliefs when giving grants for artistic projects. A federal district court upheld a law making it illegal to use computers to create pictures of children engaging in sexual conduct. A federal appellate court upheld a federal law banning the sale or rental of sexually explicit, but non-obscene, material on military bases. A federal district court overturned a law prohibiting federal prisoners from receiving publications containing "sexually explicit" material or nudity.

DEFINING OBSCENITY

Community Standard

Minors

(Insert after last paragraph, p. 354) A federal district court upheld a federal law[1] making it illegal to market as child pornography computer-generated pictures making it appear children are engaging in sexual conduct.[2] The court said the law was content-neutral because Congress was not concerned with content, but with the secondary effects of the content. Content-neutral regulations pass constitutional challenge if the government has a legitimate purpose in adopting the law. Congress said the child pornography industry and pedophiles can use computers to alter pictures of children to create images of "children engaging in

---

[1] Child Pornography Prevention Act of 1996, 18 U.S.C. §§ 2252-2256.

[2] Free Speech Coalition v. Reno, 25 Media L. Rep. (BNA) 2305 (N.D. Cal. 1997).

any imaginable form of sexual conduct." Computers also can produce such depictions without using pictures of real children. The court said reducing child pornography is a legitimate congressional purpose, saving the law from First Amendment attack.

DUE PROCESS AND PRIOR RESTRAINTS

Cutting Funds

(Insert after second paragraph, p. 363) The government may reject grant proposals for artistic projects that are indecent or do not comply with "values of the American public," the Supreme Court ruled in 1998.[3] The Court said a law requiring the National Endowment for the Arts (NEA) to consider whether artistic projects seeking federal funds show a "respect for diverse beliefs" and are "decent" does not unconstitutionally force the NEA to suppress certain viewpoints.

In 1990 Congress told the NEA to include among criteria for judging grant applications "general standards of decency and respect for the diverse beliefs and values of the American public."[4] Several artists challenged the law, arguing the statute required the NEA to engage in viewpoint discrimination by rejecting artistic projects defying mainstream values or offending generally accepted standards of decency. The 8-1 Court, disagreed, saying the law did not prevent the NEA from funding indecent artistic expression, if it chooses.

Justice Sandra Day O'Connor, writing for the majority, said there was no substantial risk the law would limit expression because the NEA does not directly apply the required criteria to each grant proposal. Rather, the NEA interprets the statute as being satisfied if panel members reviewing grant applications have diverse backgrounds and points of view. Also, the Court said, many factors go into judging the quality of artistic projects. The NEA turns down many more funding applications than it accepts, the Court said. The law only provides

---

[3] National Endowment for the Arts v. Finley, 1998 U.S. LEXIS 4211 (June 25, 1998).

[4] 20 U.S.C. § 954(d)(1).

additional criteria the NEA may use to make these decisions, according to the Court.

The Court said it was not deciding whether the NEA's method of applying the law is what Congress intended. But, the Court said, it is "clear" the law "imposes no categorical requirement" which would force the NEA to reject grant proposals because of their viewpoints. The law does no more than require the NEA "to take 'decency and respect' into consideration." Since words like "decency" and "value" are open to many interpretations, the Court said, Congress did not forbid funding specific viewpoints.

Congress "has wide latitude to set spending priorities" as long as it, or an agency it establishes, does not infringe on constitutionally protected rights, the Court said. The "decency and respect" standard does not violate the First Amendment, according to the Court.

Two members of the majority, Justices Antonin Scalia and Clarence Thomas, said the majority held the law constitutional, then made it ineffective by ignoring the law's language. Scalia said the law is very clear — the NEA must consider "respect for the diverse beliefs and values of the American public" when making grants. Scalia said the government has a right to impose these standards: "It is the very business of government to favor and disfavor points of view on (in modern times, at least) innumerable subjects ...." Scalia said the government cannot "abridge" speech. However, he said, the government has the right to fund or not fund speech based on standards in the law.

NON-OBSCENE SEXUAL EXPRESSION

(Insert after second complete paragraph, p. 364) A federal appellate court upheld a congressional ban on selling or renting sexually explicit, non-obscene materials on military bases.[5] The U.S. Court of Appeals for the Second Circuit found constitutional the 1996 Military Honor and Decency Act restricting the sale or rental of "lascivious" sexually explicit material through military exchanges —

---

[5] General Media Communications, Inc. v. Cohen, 131 F.3d 273, 26 Media L. Rep. (BNA) 1033 (2d Cir. 1997), *cert. denied,* 1998 U.S. LEXIS 4283 (June 26, 1998).

retail businesses located on military bases. The law bans sexually explicit periodicals and audio and videotapes, but not sexually explicit books. Military personnel may purchase or rent the restricted items elsewhere and are free to possess them, but the military itself, including vendors allowed on military bases, cannot sell or rent them.

The court said military exchanges are nonpublic forums because only military personnel and certain other people may make purchases there. The First Amendment, then, allows the government to restrict speech in the exchanges as long as the restriction furthers reasonable government interests and does not discriminate because of the expression's viewpoint.

The court said it was reasonable for the military to bar the sale or rental of sexually explicit materials on military bases. Congress' goal in part was to uphold the armed services' professionalism, honor, and decorum, the court agreed. Also, military bases are work places where the sale or rental of sexual materials could distract from employees efficiently performing their jobs, the court said.

The court noted the 1996 law distinguished between permitted and banned speech on the basis of sexually explicit content. But the court rejected an argument that the act discriminates against a viewpoint — that "women are sexual beings" or "the focus of sexual desire." The court said the Supreme Court allows the government to prohibit expression based on its prurience and patent offensiveness, and to do so is not viewpoint discrimination.

A U.S. district court overturned a more encompassing law preventing federal prisoners from receiving through the mail publications containing "sexually explicit" material or nudity.[6] The court said since the law did not help to rehabilitate prisoners, there was no justification for infringing prisoners' First Amendment rights.

The district court agreed rehabilitating prisoners is a legitimate goal, as the government argued before the court. But the court said rehabilitation was not Congress' purpose in adopting the ban. Rather Congress wanted to be sure

---

[6] Amatel v. Reno, 975 F. Supp. 365, 25 Media L. Rep. (BNA) 2274 (D.D.C. 1997).

prisoners were being punished, in this case by not allowing prisoners to receive publications they wanted.

9

THE MEDIA AND THE JUDICIARY

The judge who presided over Timothy McVeigh's trial on charges of bombing the Oklahoma City federal building said ensuring a fair trial was more important than public and press access to suppression motions. The McVeigh trial judge refused requests to dismiss the case, change venue, or delay the trial, saying the American justice system could withstand prejudicial publicity. The press does not have a First Amendment or common law right of access to hearings or documents connected with grand jury proceedings, a federal appellate court told journalists covering the Monica Lewinski investigation. A federal appellate court overturned a restraining order against the press in a civil case involving school desegregation. Two federal appellate courts and several federal district judges have allowed television cameras in the courtroom, but New York State did not renew its law permitting cameras in courts. A federal appellate court refused to allow journalists to interview jurors at the conclusion of a well-publicized case.

REMEDIES FOR PREJUDICIAL PUBLICITY

Continuance

(Insert before "Severance," p. 383) Judge Richard Matsch, who presided over the trial of Timothy McVeigh on charges stemming from the destruction of the Oklahoma City federal building, ruled the American criminal justice system has built-in safeguards against prejudicial publicity causing unfair trials. In 1997, McVeigh's attorneys argued news stories — in particular, reports in the *Dallas Morning News* and several other publications that McVeigh had confessed to his lawyers — had made a fair trial impossible, and asked Matsch to dismiss the indictment, grant a year's continuance, or change the venue again.

Matsch denied the requests.[1] He conceded "prodigious amounts of material addressing every angle of the story" had been published in the two years after the bombing. He also said various people, including jurors, are affected in diverse ways by what the media publish. And, the judge said, criminal trials are public by nature. But the process of criminal prosecution goes far to ensure fairness, he said. That was true in the McVeigh case particularly, from the government and the defense thoroughly investigating the facts to highly competent attorneys representing the government and the defendants, according to Matsch. He said he had "full confidence that a fair minded jury" would "return a just verdict based on the law and evidence presented to them."

The jury found McVeigh guilty of 11 counts of murder and conspiracy.[2] It recommended he be sentenced to death.[3]

CONTROLLING CONDUCT IN COURT

Cameras Move into Courtrooms

(Insert before "Summary," p. 393) Television cameras are not completely banned from federal courts. Based on the Federal Conference's decision to allow each federal circuit to decide for itself whether still and television cameras will be permitted in appellate arguments, two U.S. Courts of Appeals — the Second and Ninth Circuits — have permitted cameras in appellate arguments on a case-by-case basis.[4]

---

[1] United States v. McVeigh, 955 F. Supp. 1281 (D. Colo. 1997).

[2] Jo Thomas, "McVeigh Guilty on All Counts in the Oklahoma City Bombing; Jury to Weigh Death," *New York Times,* June 3, 1997, at A1.

[3] Jo Thomas, "McVeigh Jury Decides on Sentence of Death in Oklahoma Bombing," *New York Times,* June 14, 1997, at A1.

[4] Robert Schmidt, "Pilot Program Heads for House Vote," *Legal Times,* March 23, 1998, at 1.

After a federal district judge in the Second Circuit allowed pretrial motions to be televised,[5] the Judicial Conference issued a statement strongly urging the federal circuits to discourage permitting television cameras in courtrooms. Despite the request, two other Second Circuit district judges agreed to permit televising of pretrial motions.[6] The judges said the public interest is served best when people have an opportunity to observe courts in operation if the parties in a lawsuit will not be prejudiced.

New York State joined Indiana, Mississippi, and South Dakota as the only states banning cameras in courtrooms. The District of Columbia also forbids cameras in its courts. A 1987 New York statute permitting judges to televise judicial proceedings expired on July 1, 1997. The state legislature did not renew the law.[7]

CONTROLLING PREJUDICIAL PUBLICITY

Restraints Imposed on News Sources

(Insert after third paragraph, p. 396) A federal appellate court refused to allow journalists to interview jurors after a trial.[8] The U.S. Court of Appeals for the Fifth Circuit upheld the judge's order because it barred only juror interviews about jury deliberations in an extensively covered racketeering trial. The order did not prohibit interviews about the verdict itself, a juror's general reactions, or interviews with jurors' relatives or friends. Nor did the order prevent jurors from commenting publicly. The order restricted only interviews about discussions which took place in the jury room.

---

[5] Marisol A. v. Giuliani, 929 F. Supp. 660, 24 Media L. Rep. (BNA) 2150 (S.D.N.Y. 1996).

[6] Hamilton v. Accu-Tek, 942 F. Supp. 136 (E.D.N.Y. 1996); Katzman v. Victoria's Secret Catalogue, 923 F. Supp. 580 (S.D.N.Y. 1996).

[7] "Justice in the Dark," *New York Times,* Feb. 2, 1998, at 22.

[8] United States v. Cleveland, 128 F.3d 267, 25 Media L. Rep. (BNA) 2500 (5th Cir. 1997), *cert. denied,* 118 S. Ct. 1518 (1998).

The appellate court said journalists do not have a special First Amendment right of access to matters unavailable to the public. Because the public is not permitted to inquire about jury deliberations, the court said, neither is the press. To hold otherwise, the court said, would be to compromise jury secrecy necessary for candid discussions and private voting.

A federal appellate court held a restraining order in a civil proceeding — even one involving as important an issue as desegregating schools — violated the First Amendment.[9] After 40 years of unsuccessful attempts to comply with court-mandated integration of the East Baton Rouge, Louisiana, schools, the school board said it might achieve that goal if allowed to negotiate in private. Agreeing with the request, a federal district court directed school board members, their attorneys and certain staff members not to discuss the bargaining with others, including the press. However, the Fifth Circuit saw the order as a prior restraint on participants in the negotiating process. The appellate court said the order also might constitute a prior restraint on the news media. At minimum, the order affected the media, since it prevented them from gathering news, which they had a First Amendment right to do, the court said. The Fifth Circuit said the school board could desegregate the schools without the secrecy order, although public comment and disagreement might lengthen the process.

Access to Courtrooms

Pretrial Hearings

(Insert before "Summary," p. 414) The press has no First Amendment or common law right of access to judicial hearings or documents connected to grand jury proceedings, the U.S. Court of Appeals for the District of Columbia said.[10] The court denied media access to grand jury hearings and documents that would reveal grand jury issues or processes in the investigation of President Clinton's relationship to former White House aide Monica Lewinski. Neither the First

---

[9] Davis v. East Baton Rouge Parish School Board, 78 F.3d 920, 24 Media L. Rep. (BNA) 1513 (5th Cir. 1996).

[10] In re Motions of Dow Jones & Co., Inc., 142 F.3d 496, 26 Media L. Rep. 1660 (D.C. Cir. 1998), petition for cert. filed (June 3, 1998).

Amendment nor the common law permits violating grand jury secrecy, the court said.

The appellate court said access to the hearings or documents was governed by rules established by the federal district court overseeing the grand jury. These "local rules" allow for press access if grand jury matters will not be revealed. Journalists argued the district court did not notify the press and public when hearings connected to the Lewinski matter would be held. The press said if it did not know a hearing would be held, it could not ask for access under the local rules. The appellate court agreed and told the district court to notify the press and public when hearings related to the Lewinski investigation were scheduled.

Access to Court Records

(Insert before Summary, p. 418) A federal appellate court upheld the sealing of three groups of documents in the Terry Nichols and Timothy McVeigh Oklahoma City bombing trials.[11] The trial judge sealed Nichols' motion to suppress certain evidence, releasing only a portion of the motion. The judge also sealed reports of Nichols' nine hour statement to the FBI. Additionally, the judge sealed Nichols' and McVeigh's motions for separate trials, again permitting the press and public to see only a small part of the motion. A group of media representatives objected, claiming both a First Amendment and common law rights of access.

The U.S. Court of Appeals for the Tenth Circuit ruled against the press, using a form of the *Press-Enterprise II* test (see text, pp. 413-415). First, the appellate court said suppression motions historically have been available to the press. It is important for the press and public to have access to suppression motions, the court said, because it is at that stage when law enforcement officials' actions are under scrutiny. Second, however, the court said the press and public historically have not had access to evidence ruled inadmissible for presentation at trial. Nor is there any reason the press and public should know what evidence is inadmissible, the court said. Knowing about the inadmissible evidence will not help the public better understand the criminal justice process, the court said. Because the FBI

---

[11] United States v. McVeigh, 119 F.3d 806, 25 Media L. Rep. (BNA) 1937 (10th Cir. 1997), *cert. denied,* 118 S. Ct. 1110 (1998).

interview with Nichols consisted of hearsay that is not admissible in court, these statements also could be sealed, the court said.

The motions to try each defendant separately included trial strategies and reasons why one defendant thought the other was to blame. The trial judge properly sealed these motions, the appellate court said, because there was a "higher value" than public and press access. More important than press access was having the defendants' attorneys be candid in arguing to the court why separate trials were required. The attorneys would not be forthcoming if their arguments were disseminated by the press, constituting prejudicial pre-trial publicity.

10

PROTECTION OF NEWS SOURCES, NOTES, AND TAPE

A number of subpoenas for information are being issued to the media, particularly from the office of Independent Counsel Kenneth Starr. In one subpoena case, a federal court ordered ABC to turn over outtakes of an interview in the presidential Whitewater investigation. However, the supermarket chain, Food Lion, was barred from subpoenaing information from sources for an unflattering ABC television program. In Georgia, a judge ordered the Atlanta Journal-Constitution to reveal names and sources in the libel trial brought by Richard Jewell, once a suspect in the bombing during the 1996 Olympic games. Congress has amended the Privacy Protection Act to permit authorities to search newsrooms for child pornography.

"There seems to be an explosion of subpoenas," says media attorney Floyd Abrams.[1] The *Columbia Journalism Review* calls it "Subpoena Madness."[2] A special prosecutor investigating for4mer agriculture secretary Mike Espy subpoenaed Mike Wallace and on Hewitt, of CBS's "Sixty Minutes," to testify

---

[1]Florence George Graves, "Is This What Congress Intended?" *Washington Post,* April 12, 1998, at C1.

[2] Michael Gartner, "Subpoena Madness," Columbia Journalism Rev., July-Aug. 1998, at 45.

before a grand jury. ABC gave Independent Counsel Kenneth Starr out-takes from a Diane Sawyer interview with Clinton friend and White Water figure, Diane Sawyer. (*see this section of Update 99*) Starr backed off on a subpoena for information from William Morrow & Co. about a book by Webster Hubbell, a Clinton friend and also a figure in the White Water investigation. Facing a subpoena, Kramerbooks in Washington, D.C., agreed to turn over to Monica Lewinsky records of her book purchases so that the former White House intern could give them to Kenneth Starr for his investigation of a possible relationship between Lewinsky and the president.[3] Attorney Floyd Abrams says he knows of half dozen other subpoenas that have not been made public.

Although the frequency of subpoenas troubles the media, so, too, does the secrecy. "Everything is in a grand jury context with papers filed under seal and the information sought under seal, objections made under seal, briefings under seal," Abrams said.

PROTECTION UNDER THE FIRST AMENDMENT

Lower Court Reliance on Three Part Test

Civil Trials

(*Insert before "Journalists as Third Party, p. 439*) A federal district court in North Carolina has ruled that a supermarket chain suing the media for trespass could not subpoena information from media sources. The federal judge ruled that attempts by Food Lion to subpoena companies that had transactions with ABC during the network's undercover investigation of the supermarket chain violated the network's First Amendment right to protect confidential sources. The court granted ABC's request to stop subpoenas directed at hotels, letter carriers, and

---

[3] Stephen Labaton, "Lewinsky's Lawyers to Turn Over Records of Book Purchases," *New York Times*, June 22, 1998, at A13.

telecommunications companies that may have had communications with ABC during the investigation.[4]

The court said Food Lion was unable to show that the information sought from the third parties was crucial to its case against ABC or that it could not obtain the information from other sources. Of particular concern to the court was the breadth of the subpoenas. Food Lion was seeking all communications between the companies and ABC reporters--all personal and business communications about all subjects, including news stories unrelated to the Food Lion investigation. The court also ruled that the benefit to Food Lion was too small to justify such broad subpoenas.

Libel Suits

(*Insert before "Summary," p. 442*) In May, 1998, Georgia State Court Judge John R. Mather ordered staffers at the Atlanta Journal-Constitution to testify and provide sources in the libel case brought by Richard Jewell. Mather ruled that the Georgia shield law does not protect journalists when they are defendants in a libel case.[5] Jewell is suing the Journal-Constitution over stories published when he was a suspect in the bombing at Centennial Park during the 1996 Olympic games.

PROTECTION UNDER FEDERAL STATUTES AND REGULATIONS

(*Insert before "Summary," p. 453*) A federal court in Arkansas has ruled that ABC must turn over outtakes of an interview for a broadcast on "PrimeTime Live" about the Whitewater investigation. The federal judge ruled that ABC had no constitutional or statutory privilege to withhold outtakes from an interview with Susan McDougal, outtakes sought by Independent Counsel Kenneth W. Starr. Even if there were a qualified privilege, the court said, ABC would be required to provide the outtakes in response to a subpoena from a federal grand jury,

---

[4] Food Lion, Inc. v. Capital Cities/ABC, Inc., 24 Media L. Rep.(BNA) 2431 (M.D.N.C. 1996).

[5] Trisha Renaud and June D. Bell, "Ruling: AJC Must Tell Jewell Story Source," Fulton County Daily Report, May 1, 1998, at 1.

particularly where the grand jury had no other sources.[6] The court also ruled that the independent counsel is not bound by Department of Justice guidelines for issuing subpoenas where following the guidelines "would be inconsistent with the purpose of the statute" creating an independent counsel.

SEARCH WARRANTS

(*Insert before "Summary," p. 456*) In 1996, Congress amended the Privacy Protection Act to permit newsroom searches for child pornography. The Child Pornography Act amends the Privacy Protection Act to permit searches when the government has probable cause to believe it may find evidence of a criminal offense involving child pornography, the sexual exploitation of children, or the sale or purchase of children.[7]

---

[6]In re: Grand Jury Subpoena American Broadcasting Co., 947 F. Supp. 1314, 25 Media L. Rep. (BNA) 1235 (E.D. Ark. 1996). See, Order to Turn Over Videotape of Susan McDougal Interview," *News Media & Law*, Winter 1997, at 9.

[7]"Amendments to Privacy Protection Act Become Law," *News Media & Law*, Fall 1996, at 4.

11

ACCESS TO INFORMATION

The new Electronic Freedom of Information Act declares electronic information to be public and attempts to speed public access to federal records. The Supreme Court ruled that a federal agency does not have to provide a mailing list to an environmental group, and a federal appeals court ruled that the National Security Council is not an agency subject to open records law. But the same appeals court struck down a rigid rule under which the FBI withheld the names of agents. A federal commission proposed legislation to curb excessive classification of national security information. A federal appeals court in California ruled that the public has no constitutional right to attend executions. A new federal law limits press access at aircraft disasters. Several courts, but not all, have declared the Driver's Privacy Protection Act unconstitutional. The Ohio Supreme Court has open student judiciary records to the public.

ACCESS AND THE CONSTITUTION

Federal Lower Courts and Selective Exclusion of Journalists

(*Insert after first paragraph, p. 467*) As American prison populations rise and executions increase, many states are restricting access to prisoners and executions.[1] In 1998, the U.S. Court of Appeals for the Ninth Circuit ruled that neither the press nor the public has a First Amendment right to attend executions.[2] The appellate court upheld a San Quentin procedure allowing witnesses to view executions only after the condemned has been strapped to a gurney and an intravenous solution administered. The court overturned a lower court decision granting the press access to more of the procedure by which the state takes a condemned person's life. The lower court had ruled that the public has a First Amendment right to observe and report whether a prisoner resists, how authorities treat the condemned, and whether officials have difficulty locating a vessel to receive the executioner's needle.

Overturning the district court, the federal appeals court said the public has no First Amendment right of access to executions. The court agreed with the prison warden that exposure of the execution team to the media might result in harassment of team members and their families. The court also said that exposure to the media might jeopardize prison security.

ACCESS TO LOCATIONS OF NEWS EVENTS

Quasi-Public Property

(*Insert before "War Zones," p. 471*) A privacy law signed by President Clinton in the fall of 1996 will make it more difficult for the media to report on airplane crashes. The Aviation Disaster Family Assistance Act requires the National Transportation Safety Board to obtain from the airlines lists of passengers on downed craft and release any information only to passengers' families. The act also provides for areas where passengers can grieve in private without questions from the media. A task force will recommend ways to ensure that journalists and

---

[1] *See, e.g.*, "New State Regulations, Court Rulings Restrict Media Access to Prisons," *News Media & Law*, Spring 1997, at 14.

[2] California First Amendment Coalition v. Calderon, 138 F.3d 1298, 26 Media L. Rep. 1629 (9th Cir. 1998), *rev'g*, 956 F. Supp. 883, 25 Media L. Rep. (BNA) 1526 (N.D. Calif. 1997).

attorneys do not "intrude on the privacy of families of passengers involved in an aircraft accident."[3]

ACCESS TO RECORDS

Federal Freedom of Information Act

Defining 'Record'

(*Insert before the last full paragraph, p. 477*) In 1996, Congress enacted major legislation to extend freedom of information laws to electronic communications. The Electronic Freedom of Information Act, signed by President Clinton in October, brings electronic records into open records law and attempts to reduce the lengthy delays often endured by records requestors.[4]

EFOIA, as the electronic act is abbreviated, defines "record" to include electronic information. Under the new act, a record includes any non-exempt information maintained by an agency "in any format, including an electronic format." The new law requires agencies to make available in electronic format records that the agencies are already required to make available in hard copy. If an agency has on-line capabilities, the electronic information is to be available there. If an agency lacks on-line capacities, the agency must make the information available on CD-ROM, diskette or other electronic format.

Requesters are supposed to receive records in the format they choose, if that format is readily available. Thus, requesters should be able to receive electronic copies of databases and database queries.

EFOIA also requires federal agencies to make reasonable efforts to search for requested records in electronic form, unless a search would "significantly interfere"

---

[3]"Media Access to Information During Air Disasters Restricted," *News Media & Law*, Fall 1996, at 38.

[4]Pub. L. No. 104-231, 110 Stat. 3048, *amending* 5 U.S.C. § 552.

with agency operations. To search electronic databases, agencies may have to engage in at least limited programming. Administrators may redact electronic records, as they can paper records, to remove private, proprietary, or security information before releasing records. However, the EFOIA requires an agency to tell how much of a document, if any, has been deleted.

Allowing requesters to chose the format of records they receive overturns a federal precedent allowing administrators, not the requesters, to determine the format in which records would be released.[5] The EFOIA also challenges the Supreme Court's ruling in *Department of Justice v. Reporters Committee for Freedom of the Press* (see text, pp. 500-502) that federal records must be released only if they reveal how the government operates. Senate sponsors of EFOIA took a much broader view of the purposes of the open records law, saying that the Freedom of Information Act requires agencies to make records available to "any person for any public or private use."[6]

A study of the effectiveness of the Electronic Freedom of Information Act concluded that many federal agencies have failed to make electronic records available to the public.[7] The study by OMB Watch, a nonprofit organization involved in information policy, reported that 13 of 57 agencies had met no EFOIA requirements to allow easy public access to electronic records. Three quarters of the other agencies studied had complied with some requirements of the Electronic Freedom of Information Act, but none of them had complied completely.

Defining 'Agency'

(*Insert before "Defining Record," p. 477*) In 1996, the U.S. Court of Appeals for the District of Columbia Circuit ruled that the National Security Council, an executive branch entity with a staff of 150, is not an agency whose records are

---

[5]Dismukes v. Dept. of Interior, 603 F. Supp. 760 (D.D.C. 1984).

[6]"Will EFOIA Amendments Affect *Reporters Committee?*" *Access Rep.*, Oct. 9, 1996, at 1, 2.

[7]OMB Watch, *Government Information Insider* 2 (Winter-Spring 1998).

open under the Freedom of Information Act.[8] A federal appeals panel ruled 2-1 that the NSC is not an agency because it does not exercise substantial authority independent of the president. Because of the decision, journalist Scott Armstrong was denied thousands of electronic records he was seeking about the activities of the NSC, an entity of 150 staff members with influence in telecommunications, diplomacy, emergency preparedness, and other domestic, foreign, and military policies affecting national security.

While establishments in the Executive Office of the President may be considered "agencies," the FOIA does not cover "the President's immediate personal staff or units in the Executive Office whose sole function is to advise and assist the President." The D.C. Circuit court ruled that the National Security Council operates primarily to advise the president, not as an agency with independent authority.

The court conceded that the NSC's bureaucratic structure, large staff and separate budget made it appear more like an agency than the president's less formal personal staff. But while the bureaucratic structure might suggest the NSC is an agency, the court said the president has a close relationship to the council, much like his relationship to his personal staff. The president chairs the NSC and chooses and supervises the National Security Adviser, who oversees the staff. But most important, the court said, the NSC has little if any independent authority. Although the agency helps set policy in many areas, the court said the NSC remains a "highly personal" instrument of the president, exercising authority only with the president's direction and approval.

Response Deadlines

(*Insert before "Fees," p. 483*) To speed public access to electronic information, the Electronic Freedom of Information Act requires agencies to expedite a request where the requester has a compelling need for the records. Agencies will expedite

---

[8]Armstrong v. Exec. Office of the President, 90 F.3d 553 (D.C. Cir. 1996), *cert. denied*, 117 S. Ct. 1842 (1997).

requests when delay poses an imminent threat to an individual's life or safety or when "a person primarily engaged in disseminating information" can show an "urgency to inform the public concerning actual or alleged federal government activity."

To encourage agencies to fulfill requests within the time allowed, the EFOIA extends the time permitted for an agency response. Under EFOIA, agencies have 20 days--instead of 10 under the old law--to determine whether to grant or deny a request. If an agency cannot fulfill a request within the 20 days because of "unusual circumstances," the requester may narrow the request so that an agency can fulfill it within 20 days, or the requester and agency may negotiate a time at which the request will be fulfilled. "Unusual circumstances" are not supposed to include agency backlogs.

To speed delivery of information, agencies can abandon the usual procedure of always serving the first customer in line. Under the new law, agencies can develop multi-track policies, fulfilling simple requests quickly on one track, and more complex requests more slowly on another track. Under this plan, citizens with simple requests should not have to wait while more complex requests are being fulfilled.

Further expediting release of information, EFOIA reduces the number of formal requests that citizens must file by requiring agencies to make popular records readily available. Under EFOIA, agencies are required to make publicly available records already requested by other parties if the agency thinks the records are likely to be requested often. Within a few years, agencies must also create a Government Information Locator Service or indexes of all major information systems.

Exemptions

(1) National Security

(Insert before "(2) Agency Rules and Practices," p. 488) In March 1997, a federal commission proposed legislation to limit government information that is

classified. The commission on government secrecy, chaired by Sen. Daniel Patrick Moynihan, Democrat of New York, concluded that a "culture of secrecy" keeps too much information secret for too long.[9]

The Commission on Protecting and Reducing Government Secrecy recommended a law to authorize classification of information only where there is "a demonstrable need" to protect national security. The commission also called for a National Declassification Center to oversee the disclosure of classified information. The commission recommended declassifying most information after 10 years, and making all information public after 30 years. Senate hearings on declassification followed.

(6) Personnel, Medical, and Similar Files

(Insert before last paragraph, p. 495) In February 1997, the Supreme Court reversed a lower court ruling that the Bureau of Land Management must turn over its mailing list to an environmental group. In a brief *per curiam* opinion, the high court ruled that the U.S. Court of Appeals for the Ninth Circuit erred when it ruled that the Bureau of Land Management must reveal its mailing list to the Oregon Natural Desert Association. The Ninth Circuit had found a "substantial public interest" in allowing citizens to learn to whom the government is sending "propaganda." But the Ninth Circuit said disclosing the government mailing list would allow citizens to receive "information from other sources that do not share the [Bureau of Land Management's] self-interest in presenting government activities in the most favorable light."[10]

In its two-page opinion, the Supreme Court rebuked the Ninth Circuit for basing disclosure on a perceived public interest in providing persons on the bureau's mailing list with a different point of view. Citizens' purposes for requesting information have "no bearing" on whether information will be disclosed, the Court

---

[9]R.W. Apple, Jr., "Government Is Overzealous on Secrecy, Panel Advises," *New York Times,* Mar. 5, 1997, at A11.

[10]Bibles v. Oregon Natural Desert Ass'n, 117 S. Ct. 795 (1997).

said. Citing *Department of Defense v. Federal Labor Relations Authority* (see text, pp. 495-496), the Supreme Court reiterated that "the only relevant public interest" when a court balances the public interest in disclosure against privacy is the extent to which disclosure "would shed light on an agency's performance of its statutory duties or otherwise let citizens know what their government is up to." The Court then sent the case back to the Ninth Circuit for reconsideration.

The Supreme Court ordered no briefs and held no oral arguments before issuing its *per curiam* opinion. Furthermore, the Court has not had occasion to note that the Senate intended when it passed the Electronic Freedom of Information Act to make federal records available whether or not they reveal how the government functions.

In another case, a federal appeals court ruled that the FBI could not withhold the names of agents without balancing privacy interests against the benefits of disclosure. The U.S. Court of Appeals for the District of Columbia Circuit said the FBI must justify a categorical rule banning disclosure of all names or a decision to withhold the names of individual agents. The FBI could not simply say, without explanation, that privacy interests in withholding agents' names outweigh the public interest in disclosure, the court said.[11]

Federal Statutes Authorizing Withholding Information

Buckley Amendment

(*Insert at bottom of p. 505*) In at least two states, student judiciary records are open under state open records laws. In 1997, the Ohio Supreme Court ordered Miami University to disclose records from proceedings before the University Disciplinary Board.[12] The student newspaper, *The Miami Student*, asked for the records to develop a database and to track student crime trends. The Court said

---

[11]Armstrong v. Exec. Office of the President, 97 F.3d 575 (D.C. Cir. 1996)

[12]State Ex Rel. The Miami Student v. Miami University, 680 N.E.2d 956, 26 Media L Rep. (BNA) 1085 (Ohio 1997).

the university, when providing the disciplinary records, must include a student's age, sex, the nature of the incident, and the disciplinary penalty imposed. However, the court said information identifying a student--name, student ID, and social security number--could be withheld. The Georgia Supreme Court ruled earlier that student judiciary sessions and records at the University of Georgia were open-- including students' identifications--under the state open records act.[13]

In 1998, the federal Department of Education sued Miami University and Ohio State University to prevent them from releasing campus judiciary records containing students' names to *The Chronicle of High Education*.[14] Despite court rulings to the contrary, the Department of Education argues that judiciary records identifying students are "educational records" containing private information that a university cannot release without violating the Buckley Amendment.

In July, the Senate adopted an amendment to a higher education bill that would require universities to report attacks on public sidewalks and streets that run through campuses. Universities are already required to report crimes on campus.

Driver's Privacy Protection Act

(*Insert at bottom of p. 506*) Courts in several states have declared the Driver's Privacy Protection Act unconstitutional because Congress exceeded its authority when it required the states to administer a federal policy.[15] Congress violated the Tenth Amendment, the U.S. District Court for the District of South Carolina said, when it commanded the states to limit access to driver records, in effect forcing the states to carry out a federal policy. States, not the federal government,

---

[13]Red & Black Publishing Co. v. Bd. of Regents, 427 S.E.2d 257 (Ga. 1993).

[14] Kit Lively, "Education Department Sues to Block Release of Campus Judicial Records," *Chron. Higher Educ.*, Feb. 6, 1998, at 32.

[15] Travis v. Reno, 1998 U.S. Dist. LEXIS 8570 (W.D. Wis. 1998);); Oklahoma v. United States, 994 F. Supp. 1358, 25 Media L. Rep.(BNA) 2557 (W.D. Okla. 1997); Condon v. Reno, 972 F. Supp. 977, 25 Media L. Rep. (BNA) 2313 (D. S.C. 1997).

traditionally register motor vehicles and license individuals to drive on public roads. The Tenth Amendment provides that states retain powers not delegated to the United States government.

But a federal court in Alabama ruled that the Driver's Privacy Protection Act is constitutional.[16] The Alabama court ruled that Congress had the authority to pass the act as part of its authority to regulate interstate commerce. Congress did not unconstitutionally force a state to enforce federal policy, the court said. Rather, Congress merely regulated the states, barring them from releasing private driver information.

---

[16] Pryor v. Reno, 26 Media L. Rep (BNA) 1765 (M.D. Ala. 1998).

12

REGULATION OF BROADCASTING

The Supreme Court ruled that government-owned public television stations may exclude political candidates from debates if the decision is not based on the candidates' views. A federal appellate court ruled broadcasters could not channel into late night hours political commercials which might be "harmful to children" because they contain graphic images of aborted fetuses. Despite complaints about the quality of four Denver station's local newscasts, the FCC renewed the station's licenses saying broadcasters have broad journalistic discretion.

The FCC approved a new television program rating system, and told television set manufacturers all sets must include a v-chip by 2000 allowing families to block violent or sexual programs. The FCC set programming standards that television stations must meet to comply with the Children's Television Act, and cracked down on television broadcasters airing too many commercials during children's programs. A divided FCC refused to investigate the televising of liquor advertisements.

A federal district court required a pirate radio station to have an FCC license to stay on the air. Congress told the FCC not to require television networks to provide presidential candidates free time. The Food and Drug Administration clarified requirements for advertising prescription drugs on broadcast stations.

FEDERAL COMMUNICATIONS COMMISSION

Policy Enforcement

Licensing

(Insert before "Renewal Challenges," p. 533) A federal district court ruled operators of so-called "pirate" radio stations must acquire a broadcast license—as federal law requires—or get a waiver from the Federal Communications Commission.[1] Ending a four-year court dispute, the court said Stephen Dunifer, who ran "Free Radio Berkeley," could not operate his low power station in Northern California without a license. A federal jury in 1998 convicted another pirate station operator of broadcasting without a license.[2]

The FCC has asked dozens of pirate stations to stop operating without a license. The FCC may confiscate equipment used to broadcast illegally.

Pirate station operators claim their "micro-power" radio stations broadcast at such low power they cause no interference and therefore should require no license. Pirate operators say they have a First Amendment right to serve small areas within communities with content different than provided by large commercial stations.

The FCC must determine a station will not interfere with other broadcasters before the agency issues a license to operate.

REGULATION OF POLITICAL CANDIDATE PROGRAMMING

Access for Political Candidates

(Insert before "Summary," p. 550) Campaign reform proposals requiring television networks to give presidential candidates free time made little progress in 1998. In his January 1998 State of the Union speech, President Clinton suggested campaign spending could be curbed if broadcasters were required to give candidates free time. New Federal Communications Commission Chair William Kennard then said the FCC would consider adopting rules governing broadcast political advertisements, including free time for presidential candidates.

---

[1] United States v. Dunifer, 997 F. Supp. 1235 (N.D. Cal. 1998).

[2] Bill Coats, "Jury Convicts Lutz Radio Broadcaster," *St. Petersburg Times*, Feb. 26, 1998, at 4B.

William Kennard then said the FCC would consider adopting rules governing broadcast political advertisements, including free time for presidential candidates.

Members of Congress balked. Some congressional leaders argued the FCC did not have authority to require free time and said Congress, if necessary, would prevent the FCC from forcing networks to give away time. Some representatives threatened to cut the FCC's budget if the agency considered requiring free time.

In 1996, the FCC ruled three television networks could, but were not required to, provide free television time for major presidential candidates without violating the equal time rules. The networks proposed providing free air time ranging from a series of one-minute presentations to a one-hour broadcast. However, Section 315 might have required the networks to provide all presidential candidate with equal opportunities. The FCC said it would consider the free time to be coverage of "on-the-spot bona fide news events," and therefore exempt from Section 315 requirements.[3] Broadcasters made clear to Congress in 1998 they did not want a free time requirement.

OTHER PROGRAMMING REGULATION

Obscene, Indecent, and Profane Programming

Punishing Indecency

(Insert before "Channeling Indecency," p. 561) A federal appellate court overturned the FCC's decision to allow broadcasters to put political advertising showing pictures of aborted fetuses in the 10 p.m. to 6 a.m. time period if the broadcaster determined the graphic images would be "harmful to children."[4] The U.S. Court of Appeals for the District of Columbia Circuit said the Commission's decision would frustrate Congress' purpose in adopting Section 312(a)(7). Congress intended to provide candidates for federal office with a reasonable

---

[3] Fox Broadcasting Company, Public Broadcasting System and Capital Cities/ABC Inc., 11 FCC Red. 11101 (1996).

[4] Becker v. FCC, 95 F.3d 75 (D.C. Cir. 1996)

opportunity to reach potential voters with their messages. Federal candidates might not reach potential voters if their ads could be seen only late at night.

Also, the court said, if station personnel were to apply the "harmful to children" criterion, they would have "standardless discretion." It might be difficult in some instances to separate a broadcaster's objection to a commercial's graphic images from objections to a candidate's message, the court said. A candidate might engage in self-censorship by changing the content of a commercial to ensure it would escape being channeled into the late night hours. The court held stations are to broadcast political commercials containing graphic material just as they would advertisements without such images.

Children's Television

(Insert after last paragraph, p. 564) In 1998, the Federal Communications Commission told commercial television broadcasters they were exceeding commercial-limit requirements imposed by the 1990 Children's Television Act. The FCC reported twenty-six percent of stations seeking license renewal did not comply with the rule limiting ads in children's programs. As a remedy, the FCC said it would begin auditing stations by conducting unannounced off-air monitoring.[5] Stations found violating the rule could be reprimanded, fined, or have their license renewal endangered.

In 1996, the FCC established explicit standards for stations to use in complying with the Children's Television Act.[6] The Commission said since broadcasters had not met the law's goals of providing educational and informational programming for children, the FCC needed to establish clear guidelines. The Commission adopted rules requiring commercial and noncommercial television broadcasters to air three hours per week of "core programming." These are programs specifically designed to meet the educational and informational needs of children under 17 years old, programs shown between 7 a.m. and 10 p.m. on a regular weekly

---

[5] Mass Media Bureau Advises Commercial Television Licensees Regarding Children's Television Commercial Limits, 1998 FCC LEXIS 2398 (May 20, 1998).

[6] Children's Television Programming, 11 FCC Red. 10660 (1996).

schedule. The programs must be at least 30 minutes long. Stations not airing three hours a week of core programming may attempt to meet the Commission's requirement by broadcasting a variety of educational and informational programming, plus broadcasting appropriate public service announcements, non-weekly programs, and shows shorter than 30 minutes. At license renewal, stations meeting either set of criteria will be considered to have complied with the Children's Television Act. Stations not meeting either set of criteria fall into a third category. They must convince the FCC they meet the standards in some other way, or risk losing their licenses.

Commercials

(Insert before "Formats," p. 567) The U.S. Food and Drug Administration (FDA) clarified what information drug companies must include in radio and television prescription drug advertisements.[7] Print media prescription drug advertisements must state the drug's possible side effects and likely effectiveness. Listing side effects may require a lengthy disclosure. Since it would not be possible to include all information about side effects in a 30- or 60-second television or radio advertisement, the FDA had required stating only the major risks of taking the drug and making "adequate provision" for consumers to learn more detailed facts. But the FDA had not made clear what constituted "adequate provision."

In August 1997, the FDA announced guidelines for meeting the "adequate provision" standard. Broadcast advertisements for prescription drugs must:
    1. Include a toll-free telephone number allowing callers to request additional information by mail, e-mail, or phone;
    2. State that detailed information is available in brochures or in print advertisements;
    3. State that pharmacists or physicians can supply information; and/or
    4. Include a web page address where additional information can be found.
    The FDA will evaluate the guidelines' effectiveness in 1999 to determine whether consumers are taking advantage of the various ways to obtain information and what effects direct-to-consumer broadcast prescription drug advertisements have had on public health.

---

[7] David Stout, "Drug Makers Get Leeway on TV Ads," *New York Times,* Aug. 9, 1997, at 35.

In July 1997, the Federal Communications Commission deadlocked over a proposal to investigate liquor advertising on television. The 2-2 vote, with one Commission seat vacant, prevented the agency from undertaking an inquiry.

The proposed FCC inquiry would have investigated how many liquor advertisements are running, at what times, how likely it is children will be exposed to them, whether the FCC has jurisdiction over the ads, the First Amendment implications of the Commission regulating liquor advertising, and whether parents should be able to block the ads by using V-chip technology.[8]

For fifty years, liquor distillers had voluntarily refrained from placing commercials on broadcast television. The FCC estimates fifty television stations and some cable systems carry liquor advertisements. The broadcast television networks have refused to accept such ads. The Federal Trade Commission currently is looking into questions involving televised liquor advertisements.

Distorted or Staged News

(Insert after the first full paragraph under "Distorted or Staged News," p. 568)
Broadcast licensees have a wide latitude of journalistic discretion, the Federal Communications Commission affirmed in 1998.[9] The First Amendment and the Communications Act prohibit the FCC from interfering with licensee decisions about what to include in local newscasts, a Commission bureau ruled. Complaints from a watchdog group that four Denver television stations stereotyped minorities and women, included large amounts of "fluff" in their local news programs, and devoted half of their newscasts to crime and disasters would not support denying license renewals, the FCC's Mass Media Bureau said.

The Rocky Mountain Media Watch analyzed the Denver stations' newscasts during one to five day periods from 1994 through early 1997. The organization

---

[8] John M. Broder, "Tie Vote Blocks F.C.C. Inquiry on Liquor Ads," New York Times, July 10, 1997, at A20; "FCC Rejects Launching Liquor Ad Inquiry on Expᵉcted 2-2 Vote," Communications Daily, July 10, 1997.

[9] Applications for Renewal of Licenses of Television Stations at Denver, Colorado, 1998 FCC LEXIS 2089 (Apr. 30, 1998) (Mass Media Bureau).

said stations ignored important issues while devoting a third of their newscasts to soft feature stories and half to sensational crime, disaster, war, and terrorism stories. The group also said people of color, particularly African-American men, were shown as criminals and white women were portrayed as crime victims. Women and minorities were under-represented as leaders and authorities, the report said, but white men were news anchors, reporters, and sources. The stations denied the charges and said Media Watch's studies lacked scientific accuracy.

The FCC bureau denied the group's demand for limited license renewal or requiring the stations to engage in public education campaigns about the shortcomings of television news. The bureau said the Commission assumes licensees' editorial judgments are made in good faith. Licensees have broad discretion in selecting programs and deciding on the content of local shows, the bureau said. Both the First Amendment the Communications Act prevent the FCC from interfering with program decisions, the bureau said.

Only when a broadcaster is unreasonable or discriminatory in its selection of issues to cover may the FCC take action, the bureau said. The bureau also said the stations complied with the Commission's equal employment opportunity guidelines, nullifying Media Watch's complaint about the predominance of white men as newscasters.

Violence, Hoaxes, and Fraud

Violence

(Insert before "Hoaxes," p. 571) In March 1998, the Federal Communications Commission gave final approval to the television program ratings system broadcasters, the cable industry, and the Motion Picture Association of America developed.[10] The ratings, assigned to all television programs except news and sports, alert parents to program material they may not want their children to watch. The ratings also may be used in conjunction with v-chips installed in television sets. V-chip technology reads ratings encoded in programs and can block the programs' reception.

---

[10] Video Program Ratings, 13 FCC Rcd. 8232 (1998).

The ratings are:

Programs designed for children:

TV-Y	Appropriate for all children
TV-Y7	Programs directed to children seven years old and above
TV-Y7-FV	Fantasy violence may not be appropriate for seven-year-old children

Programs designed for general audiences:

TV-G	For general audiences
TV-PG	Parental guidance suggested; the program may contain material unsuitable for younger children. The program also may contain: (V), moderate violence; (S) some sexual scenes; (L), occasional coarse language; or (D), some suggestive dialogue.
TV-14	Parents strongly cautioned; the program may contain material unsuitable for children under 14 years of age. The program also may contain: (V), intense violence; (S) intense sexual scenes; (L), strong coarse language; or (D), intensely suggestive dialogue.
TV-MA	Mature audiences only; the program may contain material unsuitable for children under 17 years of age. The program also may contain: (V), graphic violence; (S) explicit sexual scenes; (L), strong coarse language.

Congress included the ratings system requirement in the Telecommunications Act of 1996.[11] All major broadcast and cable television networks except NBC and Black Entertainment Television rate their programs for age group suitability and content, such as violence or sexual material. NBC and Black Entertainment Television use age group, but not content, ratings.

---

[11] Pub. L. No. 104-104, § 551,110 Stat. 56 (1996); 47 U.S.C. §§ 303, 330.

In 1998, the television industry established an Oversight Monitoring Board charged with ensuring television program ratings are accurate and consistent. The board includes members from broadcast television, cable television, program production companies, and the public. The board has no enforcement power except public pressure.

The Telecommunications Act of 1996 also requires television receivers with thirteen inch or larger screens to include v-chips. In 1998, the FCC said v-chips must be installed in half the television receivers made for sale in the United States by July 1, 1999, and in all sets by January 1, 2000.[12] The dates each are a year later than the FCC originally ordered.

NONCOMMERCIAL BROADCASTING

Program Choices

(Insert before "Advertising," p. 577) Government-owned public broadcast stations may exclude candidates from debates as long as the exclusions are not made on the basis of a candidate's views, the U.S. Supreme Court held in 1998.[13] A public station may limit debate participants to candidates who are viable and "serious" without infringing the First Amendment rights of candidates not invited to participate, the Court said.

The Court upheld the decision of the Arkansas Educational Television Commission (AETC) to invite only major party candidates and others "who had strong popular support" to participate in a 1992 debate. Independent candidate Ralph Forbes, who was not included, sued AETC, claiming his First Amendment rights were abridged. The U.S. Court of Appeals for the Eighth Circuit ruled for Forbes, saying he could be excluded only if AETC had a compelling reason.[14]

---

[12] Technical Requirements to Enable Blocking of Video Programming Based on Program Ratings, 1998 FCC LEXIS 1246 (March 12, 1998).

[13] Arkansas Educational Television Commission v. Forbes, 118 S. Ct. 1633, 26 Media L. Rep. (BNA) 1673 (1998).

[14] Forbes v. Arkansas Educational Television Communication Network Foundation, 93 F.3d 497, 24 Media L. Rep. (BNA) 2295 (8th Cir. 1996).

Ruling that political debates on public television are not a public forum, the Court said that journalists need not demonstrate a compelling interest to justify excluding candidates the journalists consider "unewsworthy." As long as the publicly funded stations do not try to stifle a particular point of view, they may exercise editorial discretion when broadcasting debates among political candidates, the Court said.

Operating a non-public forum, broadcasters can limit participants in political debates to "serious" candidates from "major" parties. The Court said AETC did not violate Forbes' First Amendment rights when it denied him a place in the candidates' debate because he had no chance to win. The Court said the station's decision to exclude Forbes as based on viewpoint neutral journalistic discretion, not on an unconstitutional judgment to exclude Forbes because of his political views.

Any other result could lead the approximately 230 government-supported public television stations not to carry any candidate debates, the Court said. For example, the Court said, after the U.S. Court of Appeals for the Eighth Circuit ruled AETC was wrong in not including Forbes, the Nebraska Educational Television Network canceled a debate among U.S. Senate candidates because of concerns even minor candidates had to be included.

In dissent, Justice John Paul Stevens, also writing for Justices Ruth Bader Ginsburg and David Souter, said AETC used "standardless" criteria in deciding to exclude Forbes. Stevens said AETC is a government agency and those who decided not to invite Forbes were government employees. Stevens said "pre-established, objective criteria" must be applied when the government is so intimately involved in choosing who may use a government forum to speak.

In 1996, the U.S. Court of Appeals for the Eighth Circuit ruled publicly-funded noncommercial stations need not include minor party candidates in televised debates if they believe the candidates are not "newsworthy."[15] The court held ordering an Iowa public television station to include third-party congressional

---

[15] Marcus v. Iowa Public Television, 97 F.3d 1137, 24 Media L. Rep. (BNA) 2514 (8th Cir. 1996).

candidates in a debate would interfere with the station's "editorial integrity" and "editorial discretion" in carrying out its "primary mission of serving the public." The court said since the state funded the station, it was a government agency. Therefore, the station must provide a compelling interest to justify preventing the minor party candidates' from appearing. The court said the station had stated such an interest — limiting access to only "newsworthy" candidates as a way to meet the station's "public service goals."

13

REGULATION OF CABLE TELEVISION, TELEPHONE, AND NEW ELECTRONIC MEDIA

The Supreme Court, giving the Internet full First Amendment protection, held the Communications Decency Act violated the First Amendment. Also, the Court upheld the must-carry rules which require most cable operators to put local television stations on their systems. The Court affirmed a special three-judge federal district court ruling that cable operators must completely scramble or block channels carrying predominantly adult programming, or show such programming only from 10 p.m. to 6 a.m. A federal district court held a cable operator's First Amendment rights are abridged if a city attempts to force a system to carry a specific cable network.

Public libraries blocking Internet sites must have compelling reasons and use narrowly tailored methods, a federal court ruled. A New York court said only Congress, not state legislatures, should regulate the Internet. Members of Congress have introduced bills requiring blocking software on school and public library computers. A federal appellate court said the country's largest telephone companies cannot engage in electronic publishing until 2000.

CABLE

Cable and the First Amendment

Constitutionality of Cable Programming Regulations

(Insert before "Privacy Protection for Subscribers," p. 595) A city cannot require a cable operator to carry a specific cable network, even on government access channels, a federal district court ruled in late 1996.[1] The court ruled New York City could not force Time Warner, which operates most of the cable systems in the city, to carry Fox News Channel, a competitor to Time Warner's newly acquired Cable News Network (CNN). The court said the city unconstitutionally violated Time Warner's "editorial autonomy" by trying to require the operator to carry Fox News on the city's access channel.

New York City officials feared Fox might balk at fulfilling a deal to provide nearly 4,000 jobs at its New York studios if the city's major cable systems failed to carry Fox News. Personality conflicts between some executives at Time Warner and Fox News also were involved.

The court said the city's attempt to force Time Warner to carry Fox News was an unconstitutional punishment for Time Warner's refusal to run the news network. The city's coercion, the court said, violated Timed Warner's editorial autonomy.

The court said the 1984 cable act did not allow New York City to carry Fox News on the city's government access channel as the city tried to do. Congress wanted cable operators to provide channels which would show local government at work, the court said. The cable act provision would be meaningless if a government could use the access channel for any purpose, such as providing commercial programming in competition with the cable operator's own program offerings, the court said.

Time Warner and Fox News settled the dispute in July 1997. Time Warner will carry the Fox News network on its New York City cable systems and, in the next few years, on some other United States cable systems Time Warner owns. In

---

[1]Time Warner Cable v. City of New York, 943 F. Supp. 1357 (S.D.N.Y. 1996).

return, Time Warner will gain access to satellite television services owned by News Corporation, Fox News's corporate parent, in several other countries.[2]

(Substitute from last paragraph, p. 598, through second complete paragraph, p. 601) The *Turner* case returned to the Supreme Court after 18 months of fact-finding and another decision by a special three-judge federal district court. This time, the Supreme Court decided the so-called must-carry rules,[3] requiring most cable operators to transmit local television broadcast signals, do not violate the First Amendment.[4] The Court majority found the regulation was content-neutral and narrowly drawn. The Court said the government justified the regulation by showing substantial interests, and the must-carry rules did not excessively burden cable operators' free speech.

Confirming its earlier *Turner* decision, the majority saw must carry as a content-neutral economic regulation preventing "cable operators from exploiting their economic power to the detriment of broadcasters." The majority said the must-carry rules are not a content regulation "distinguish[ing] favored speech from disfavored speech on the basis of the ideas or views expressed." Must-carry, the Court said, ensures "that all Americans, especially those unable to subscribe to cable, have access to free television programming — whatever its content."

Because must-carry is a content-neutral regulation, the government does not have to justify it with a compelling reason, but must meet an intermediate level of scrutiny, the Court noted. A content-neutral law is constitutional if shown to further an important or substantial governmental interest unrelated to the suppression of free speech, provided the incidental restrictions do not "burden substantially more speech than is necessary to further" those interest (see text, pp. 67-71).

---

[2] Thomas J. Luech, "Deal with Time Warner Would Bring Fox News to the City by October," *New York Times*, July 24, 1997, at B5.

[3] 47 U.S.C § 534.

[4] Turner Broadcasting System, Inc. v FCC, 520 U.S. 180, 25 Media L. Rep. (BNA) 1449 (1997).

In its 1994 decision, the Court said it needed more facts to determine if the government's alleged interests were substantial. In 1997, the Court decided a detailed record of possible harm to broadcasters in the absence of must carry justified the legislation. The Court again split 5-4, with Justice Breyer's concurring opinion being the deciding vote. The primary Court opinion, written by Justice Kennedy, said must-carry furthers three government interests. First, must-carry ensures local over-the-air television broadcasting will survive. Second, the Court said, it furthers dissemination of information and views from a wide variety of sources. Third, Justice Kennedy said, must-carry promotes fair competition among television program providers. Justice Breyer, who agreed survival of broadcast television and a multiplicity of information sources were important government interests, did not agree fair competition between cable and broadcast television was a justifiable concern.

The Supreme Court was satisfied that without must-carry cable system operators might jeopardize over-the-air broadcasting — including original programming — by some television stations. The Court stressed that in 1992, forty percent of television households in the United States did not take cable, and therefore depended on over-the-air stations. Congress said, and the Court agreed, that without cable subscribers as viewers the stations might not attract sufficient advertising to maintain their quality, or even to stay on the air.

The Court said cable operators have incentives to drop broadcast stations since cable systems compete with broadcasters for advertising. Cable operators could prefer to carry cable programming in which they have investments rather than carrying the programming of broadcast stations. The Court cited evidence that stations which had been denied cable access had lost revenues and, in some instances, declared bankruptcy. The Court said it was not necessary for Congress to show the entire television broadcasting industry would collapse in the absence of must-carry. The loss of individual television stations would deprive viewers without cable of access to a multiplicity of views.

Finally, the Court determined must-carry does not burden cable operators' and cable programmers' First Amendment rights substantially more than necessary to further the government's interests. The Court cited evidence that cable operators generally have met their must-carry obligations without having to drop any cable programming. Also, the Court said, cable systems would carry most, although not all, television stations even without being required to.

(Insert before "Summary," p. 604) A special three-judge federal district court ruled Congress did not violate cable programmers' First Amendment rights by adopting a law to ensure adult programming cannot accidentally be seen in homes not subscribing to it.[5] In the Telecommunications Act of 1996 Congress required cable television system operators to completely scramble or block the audio and video signals of any channel showing predominantly adult programming.[6] These channels' signals sometimes "bleed" because of incomplete scrambling, so those who do not subscribe to them — including children — might see or hear a portion of the programs. Any cable system unable to make the signals completely unavailable to non-subscribers would be permitted to carry channels with adult programming only during the FCC's "safe harbor" hours of 10 p.m. to 6 a.m.

In upholding the law, the court said the statute was not aimed at the adult-oriented speech itself, but at the problem of ensuring such programming not enter cable subscribers' homes when it is not wanted. Nonetheless, because the law concerns only adult-oriented material, the court decided to treat the statute as content-based, requiring a compelling governmental interest and a narrowly tailored law.

The compelling interest is to protect children from being exposed to adult programming, the court said. And the law is narrowly tailored to achieve that end by giving system operators the choice of scrambling or channeling the program into safe harbor hours. The Supreme Court affirmed the decision without writing an opinion to explain its reasons.

---

[5] Playboy Entertainment Group, Inc. v. United States, 918 F. Supp. 813, 24 Media L. Rep. (BNA) 1522 (D. Del. 1996), *injunction denied,* Playboy Entertainment Group, Inc. v. United States, 945 F. Supp. 772 (D. Del. 1996), *aff'd without opinion,* 117 S. Ct. 1309 (1997).

[6] 104 Pub. L. 104, § 505, 110 Stat. 56 (1996).

TELEPHONE

Regulation of Telephone Company Distribution of Information and Entertainment

Other Content-Related Regulation

(Insert before the first complete paragraph, p. 609) The country's largest telephone companies cannot provide electronic publishing until February 8, 2000, a federal appeliate court ruled in 1998. [7] The court rejected arguments a federal ban abridged the phone companies' First Amendment rights. Congress included the restriction in the Telecommunications Act of 1990.[8] The law says the phone companies cannot publish or sell news, sports, entertainment, business, financial, editorial, advertising, photographic, research, literary, or scientific materials until the restriction expires in 2000. The statute prevents former Bell telephone companies from providing customers news and information through any means, including broadcast stations, cable television, print media, and the Internet.

The U.S. Court of Appeals for the District of Columbia said neither Congress nor the Federal Communications Commission, which implemented the congressional statute, limited the phone companies' speech by censoring certain viewpoints. The court said the publishing ban was a content-neutral business regulation promotion competition by preventing phone companies from using telephone service profits to underwrite publishing businesses.

Restrictions on Telephone Users

Regulation of Sexually Oriented Content

(Substitute from first paragraph, p. 613, to subhead, p. 614) In a decision striking down the Communications Decency Act (see text, p. 612), the U.S. Supreme

---

[7] BellSouth Corp. v. FCC, 1998 U.S. App. LEXIS 9769 (D.C. Cir. 1998).

[8] 47 U.S.C. § 274.

Court said the Internet should receive expansive First Amendment protection.[9] The Court said laws limiting Internet content must be analyzed under a "strict scrutiny" standard (see text, p. 33). Less stringent standards applied to broadcasting regulations are not applicable to the Internet, the Court said.

In *Reno v. ACLU,* Justice Stevens, writing for the 7-2 Court majority, said the CDA abridged adults' free speech in an attempt to prevent children from being exposed to indecent material on the Internet. The CDA criminalized using computers to display "patently offensive material" to minors. The law also made it illegal to use the Internet to knowingly send children "indecent" material.

The Court found the CDA was overbroad because it criminalized communications which are constitutionally protected. For example, material on the Internet which has literary, artistic, political, or scientific value would be illegal under the act, said the Court, although the material is protected for adults if published in other media. While the *Miller* obscenity test shelters sexual speech with social value (see text, pp. 356-357), the CDA did not. Justice Stevens said the CDA might have penalized otherwise protected messages about birth control, homosexuality, prison rape, or the First Amendment.

The Court said the CDA also was overbroad because individual communities were allowed to define terms such as "indecent" and "patently offensive." Since the Internet is a national communications medium, the Court said, any Internet message could be received in the country's most conservative community. The Court said the community using the narrowest, most confining definitions would set the standard for the entire country.

Communities were left to define "patently offensive" and "indecent" because Congress did not clearly define them, the Court said. The word "indecent" is not defined in the law at all. The term "patently offensive" is defined as material involving "sexual or excretory activities or organs" as taken "in context" and "measured by contemporary community standards." The Court said these phrases meant to give context to "patently offensive" are themselves not defined. Without

---

[9] Reno v. ACLU, 117 S. Ct. 2329 (1997).

clear definitions, the Court said, the words "will provoke uncertainty among speakers about ... just what they mean."

Although the Supreme Court had defined "indecency" in *FCC v. Pacifica Foundation* (see text, pp. 557-559), the *Reno v. ACLU* Court said *Pacifica* was not applicable to the Internet. In *Pacifica,* the Supreme Court held the FCC could ban indecent material on radio and television except during hours when children were not likely to be in the audience.

The Court stressed the Internet's "unique" nature. The Court said at any given time tens of thousands of people are discussing a "huge range of subjects." Internet content "is as diverse as human thought," the Court said. The Court recognized the Internet's is used as a worldwide soap box. The Internet, then, is different from broadcasting, the Court said. Limited spectrum space makes broadcast frequencies scarce. But there is no physical limitation on the Internet preventing users from sending messages, the Court said.

Also, courts have found broadcasting to be "invasive" because radio and television broadcasting enter the home for free at all hours. A person changing to a different station or channel may be exposed to offensive material inadvertently. Gaining access to the Internet requires a user to take deliberate actions, from turning on the computer, to connecting to an Internet server, to entering a specific site name.. The Court said because certain steps must be taken, it is unlikely an Internet user accidentally would encounter indecent material.

The Supreme Court rejected the government's argument that several earlier Court decisions made the CDA should constitutional. For instance, the Court said the *Ginsberg v. New York* decision (see text, pp. 353-354) did not apply to the CDA. In *Ginsberg* the Court upheld a New York State law making it illegal to sell minors material not obscene for adults. Unlike *Ginsberg,* the CDA would have punished knowingly providing indecent Internet material to children — even with their parents' consent or participation. Also unlike *Ginsberg,* the CDA prohibited material having redeeming social importance.

The Court also said *City of Renton v. Playtime Theatres* (see text, pp. 364-365) was not applicable to the Internet. The Court said the law in *Renton* was intended to prevent secondary effects of adult theaters, such as crime and lowered property values. The CDA, said the Court, was a content-based statute, directly restricting speech.

The Court acknowledged the government's interest in protecting children from indecent material. The Court said parental control or software which blocks certain content would be a constitutionally acceptable way to prevent access to indecent material. The Court majority left open the possibility of finding constitutional a more precisely and narrowly drawn statute. Justice O'Connor, joined by Chief Justice Rehnquist in a partial dissent, specifically encouraged Congress to rewrite the CDA.

(Insert before "Other Content Regulation," p. 614) Legislators and other public officials continue trying to control Internet content — generally without success. In 1998, a federal district court ruled in 1998 public libraries must have a compelling reason to limit access to certain Internet sites and must narrowly tailor restrictions so no constitutionally protected sites are blocked.[10] While prohibiting access to obscene content and child pornography on the Internet is justified, blocking material "harmful to minors" may prevent adults having access to protected speech, the court said.

A Virginia public library system used commercially available software on all its publicly accessible computers, blocking access to child pornography, obscene material, and content harmful to juveniles. Plaintiffs, a group of library users, said the software was intended to block sites "harmful to children," but also blocked such sites as the Quaker Home Page and the American Association of University Women-Maryland site.

The court said First Amendment standards apply when public libraries impose content-based limits on Internet access. The government must have a compelling

---

[10] Mainstream Loudoun v. Board of Trustees of the Loudoun County Library, 26 Media L. Rep. (BNA) 1609 (E.D. Va. 1998).

interest to impose content-based restrictions, and the restrictions must be narrowly tailored to achieve the government's goal, the court said. The Supreme Court's *Reno v. ACLU* decision[11] applied this standard to the Internet, according to the district court.

The library argued its reason for blocking sites was to protect children. The court agreed obscene material and child pornography are not protected expression and the library may block access to such content. However, content "deemed harmful to juveniles" may include material acceptable for adults. The Supreme Court in *Reno* and other cases has said the government may not limit what is available to adults in the interest of protecting children, the district court said.

The district court said the library's software blocked some sites protected for adults and other sites with no sexual content at all. Also, the court said, in selecting sites to block the software manufacturer uses secret criteria "which may or may not bear any relation to legal definitions of obscenity or child pornography." The government must use a narrowly tailored method when restricting speech based on its content, the court said. The library's software sweeps too broadly, the court said.

The library claimed its "unblocking" procedure made its restrictive access policy constitutional. A library patron could submit a written request for access, including name, telephone number, and a thorough explanation why access was sought. The library staff then could choose to grant access. The court found this method violated the First Amendment. It required a library patron to take action— completing a request form — to exercise First Amendment rights. Also, the system could chill First Amendment rights since some patrons may not wish to publicly state they want access to Internet sites a government agency disapproves. Finally, the library staff had unlimited discretion to grant or refuse access, based on no clear standards.

Bills introduced in both houses of Congress in 1998 would require schools and libraries receiving federal funds to install blocking software on computers

---

[11] 117 S. Ct. 2329, 25 Media L. Rep. (BNA) 1833 (1997).

available to minors.[12] Sen. John McCain's (R-Ariz.) and Rep. Robert D. Franks' (R-N.J.) proposed legislation would withhold federal funds from libraries and elementary and secondary schools which have Internet access but do not implement a method of filtering materials deemed inappropriate for minors. Both bills forbid federal intervention in choosing what Internet sites to block, leaving decisions to local officials. The bills also instruct the Federal Communications Commission to study blocking systems' effectiveness.

A New York State court said a law making it criminal to use the Internet to transmit "actual or simulated nudity, sexual conduct or sado-masochistic abuse which is harmful to minors" breached the U.S. Constitution's Commerce Clause.[13] The state court said only Congress can regulate the Internet because it is a national and international area of commerce.

---

[12] Internet School Filtering Act, S. 1619, 105th Cong., 2d Sess. (1998); Safe Schools Internet Act, H.R. 3177, 105th Cong., 2d Sess. (1998).

[13] American Library Association v. Pataki, 969 F. Supp. 160, 25 Media L. Rep. (BNA) 2217 (S.D.N.Y.

The state law was not limited to activities entirely within New York, the court said. The law could be applied anywhere. For example, the statute's sweep could snare a university art historian in Florida transmitting a painting of a nude woman. The court said because Internet data may pass through computers located outside the state — even when a New York resident communicates with another New York resident — the state legislature could not confine the law's reach to activities only within New York State.

The state court said protecting children against pedophilia is a legitimate state goal. However, the court said, the likelihood the law will be effective is small, while the impact on interstate commerce — the development of the Internet — would be large. Also, the court said, if one state adopts a law punishing Internet content, other could adopt inconsistent laws. This would inhibit Internet growth. To avoid this problem, only Congress should pass Internet legislation, the court said.